E-mail
on the
Internet

BOOKS AVAILABLE

By both authors:

BP306 A Concise Introduction to Ami Pro 3
BP327 DOS one step at a time
BP337 A Concise User's Guide to Lotus 1-2-3 for Windows
BP341 MS-DOS explained
BP343 A concise introd'n to Microsoft Works for Windows
BP346 Programming in Visual Basic for Windows
BP351 WordPerfect 6 explained
BP352 Excel 5 explained
BP353 WordPerfect 6.0 for Windows explained
BP354 Word 6 for Windows explained
BP362 Access one step at a time
BP372 CA-SuperCalc for Windows explained
BP387 Windows one step at a time
BP388 Why not personalise your PC
BP399 Windows 95 one step at a time*
BP400 Windows 95 explained*
BP402 MS Office one step at a time
BP405 MS Works for Windows 95 explained
BP406 MS Word 95 explained
BP407 Excel 95 explained
BP408 Access 95 one step at a time
BP409 MS Office 95 one step at a time
BP415 Using Netscape on the Internet
BP419 Using Microsoft Explorer on the Internet
BP420 E-mail on the Internet
BP426 MS-Office 97 explained
BP428 MS-Word 97 explained
BP429 MS-Excel 97 explained
BP430 MS-Access 97 one step at a time

By Noel Kantaris:

BP232 A Concise Introduction to MS-DOS
BP258 Learning to Program in C
BP259 A Concise Introduction to UNIX*
BP261 A Concise Introduction to Lotus 1-2-3
BP264 A Concise Advanced User's Guide to MS-DOS
BP274 A Concise Introduction to SuperCalc 5
BP284 Programming in QuickBASIC
BP325 A Concise User's Guide to Windows 3.1

E-mail
on the
Internet

by

P.R.M. Oliver
and
N. Kantaris

BERNARD BABANI (publishing) LTD
THE GRAMPIANS
SHEPHERDS BUSH ROAD
LONDON W6 7NF
ENGLAND

PLEASE NOTE

Although every care has been taken with the production of this book to ensure that any projects, designs, modifications and/or programs, etc., contained herewith, operate in a correct and safe manner and also that any components specified are normally available in Great Britain, the Publishers and Author(s) do not accept responsibility in any way for the failure (including fault in design) of any project, design, modification or program to work correctly or to cause damage to any equipment that it may be connected to or used in conjunction with, or in respect of any other damage or injury that may be so caused, nor do the Publishers accept responsibility in any way for the failure to obtain specified components.

Notice is also given that if equipment that is still under warranty is modified in any way or used or connected with home-built equipment then that warranty may be void.

© 1997 BERNARD BABANI (publishing) LTD

First Published – May 1997
Reprinted – August 1998

British Library Cataloguing in Publication Data:

A catalogue record for this book is available from the British Library

ISBN 0 85934 420 7

Cover Design by Gregor Arthur
Cover illustration by Adam Willis
Printed and Bound in Great Britain by Cox & Wyman Ltd, Reading

ABOUT THIS BOOK

E-mail on the Internet has been written to help you get to grips with both e-mail and the Internet. These days you can't read a paper, listen to a request show on the radio, or watch television very long before you hear or see mention of e-mails or of the Internet. This communication medium has certainly become an integral part of our lives over the last few years. Hence the reason for the book.

An attempt has been made not to use too much computer 'jargon', but with this subject, some is inevitable, so a glossary of terms is included, which should be used with the text where necessary.

To set the scene, the book starts with a very short history of e-mail and the Internet. If you don't want to read this sort of thing, you can skip these few pages!

The next chapter dives in at the deep end with an explanation of what you will need to get up and running with e-mails on the Internet. This includes the hardware, your Internet connection and the type of software that is available, free of charge.

Chapters follow describing the Windows 95 versions of four of the most popular e-mail programs that are freely available on the Internet. The format of each of these chapters follows the same lines, with the idea being that you should try each before deciding which program to use for your e-mail work. We do not recommend that you sit down and read these four chapters one after the other!

One thing to remember when reading the book is that the whole Internet scenario is changing every day, especially the World Wide Web. What is there to look at today, may have gone, or changed shape, by tomorrow. Hopefully the sites we point to in our text will still be there, but there are no guarantees.

The book does not describe how to set up your PC, or how to use Windows 95 itself. If you need to know more about the Windows environment, then we suggest you select an appropriate level book from the 'Books Available' list at the beginning of this section. These books are loosely graduated in complexity from the less demanding *one step at a time* series, to the more detailed *explained* series. They are all published by BERNARD BABANI (publishing) Ltd.

Like the rest of our computer series, this book was written with the busy person in mind. It is not necessary to learn all there is to know about a subject, when reading a few concise pages can usually do the same thing quite adequately. With the help of this book, it is hoped that you will be able to come to terms with e-mail and the Internet and get the most out of your computer, and that you will be able to do it in the shortest, most effective and informative way. Good luck, and most important, enjoy.

If you would like to purchase a Companion Disc for any of the listed books by the same author(s), **apart from this book and the ones marked with an asterisk**, containing the file/program listings which appear in them, then fill in the form at the back of the book and send it to Phil Oliver at the address given.

ABOUT THE AUTHORS

Phil Oliver graduated in Mining Engineering at Camborne School of Mines in 1967 and since then has specialised in most aspects of surface mining technology, with a particular emphasis on computer related techniques. He has worked in Guyana, Canada, several Middle Eastern countries, South Africa and the United Kingdom, on such diverse projects as: the planning and management of bauxite, iron, gold and coal mines; rock excavation contracting in the UK; international mining equipment sales and international mine consulting for a major mining house in South Africa. In 1988 he took up a lecturing position at Camborne School of Mines (part of Exeter University) in Surface Mining and Management.

Noel Kantaris graduated in Electrical Engineering at Bristol University and after spending three years in the Electronics Industry in London, took up a Tutorship in Physics at the University of Queensland. Research interests in Ionospheric Physics, led to the degrees of M.E. in Electronics and Ph.D. in Physics. On return to the UK, he took up a Post-Doctoral Research Fellowship in Radio Physics at the University of Leicester, and then in 1973 a lecturing position in Engineering at the Camborne School of Mines, Cornwall, (part of Exeter University), where since 1978 he has also assumed the responsibility for the Computing Department.

ACKNOWLEDGEMENTS

We would like to thank colleagues at the Camborne School of Mines for the helpful tips and suggestions which assisted us in the writing of this book. We would also like to thank the staff of Qualcomm Inc, for sending us their most recent software.

TRADEMARKS

CONTENTS

1. SETTING THE SCENE

What is E-mail

E-mail, or electronic mail, is a cheaper, quicker, and usually much easier way, to prepare and send messages than Post Office mail. So what is an e-mail? It's simply an electronic message sent between computers. It can include attachments like pictures, document files or even Web pages. The message is passed from one computer to another as it travels through the Internet, with each computer reading its e-mail address and routing it further until it reaches its destination, where it is stored in a 'mailbox'. This usually only takes a few minutes, and sometimes only seconds.

As long as you have a computer and can access the Internet you can use e-mail for keeping in touch with friends and family and for professional reasons. You can send e-mail to most people, anywhere in the world, as long as they have their own e-mail address. These days all Internet service providers offer an e-mail address and mailbox facility to all their customers. A mailbox, as its name suggests, is simply a storage area which holds your incoming messages until you are ready to look at them. Without this they would have nowhere to go whenever your own computer was switched off.

To retrieve your e-mail messages you have to contact your mailbox, download them to your PC, and then read and process them (just like any other mail).

As we shall see, there are many packages, most of them freely available, that make this whole procedure very easy and that take most of the mystery out of the whole e-mail process. Downloading of your mail can be automatically done for you, if the e-mail package is correctly set up.

What is the Internet? - A Brief History

In the mid 1960's with the cold war very prominent in the Northern Hemisphere, the US military faced a strange strategic problem. How could the country successfully communicate after a possible nuclear war? They would need a command and control communication network linking the cities, states and military bases, etc. But, no matter how the network was protected it would always be vulnerable to the impact of a nuclear attack and if the network had a control centre it would be the first to go.

As a solution, the concept was developed that the network itself should be assumed to be unreliable at all times and should be designed to overcome this unreliability. To achieve this, all the nodes of the network would be equal in status, each with its own authority to originate, pass, and receive messages. The messages themselves would be divided into small parts, or packets, with each being separately addressed. The transmission of each packet of data would begin at a specified source node, and end at another specified destination node, but would find its own way through the network, with the route taken being unimportant. With this concept, if sections of the network were destroyed, that wouldn't matter as the packets would use the surviving nodes.

The National Physical Laboratory, here in the UK, set up the first test network on these principles in 1968. Shortly afterwards, the Pentagon's Advanced Research Projects Agency (ARPA) funded a larger, more ambitious project in the USA, with the high-speed 'supercomputers' of the day as the network nodes.

In 1969, the first such node was installed in UCLA. By December of that year, there were four nodes on the infant network, which was named ARPANET, after its sponsor. The four computers could transfer data on dedicated high-speed transmission lines, and could be programmed remotely from the other nodes. For

2

the first time, scientists and researchers could share one another's computer facilities from a long distance. By 1972 there were thirty-seven nodes in ARPANET.

The Origins of E-mail:

It soon became apparent, however, that much of the traffic on ARPANET was not long-distance computing, but consisted of news and personal messages. Researchers were using ARPANET not only to collaborate on projects and to exchange ideas on work, but to socialise. They had their own personal accounts on the ARPANET computers, and their own personal addresses for electronic mail and they were very enthusiastic about this particular new service, which we shall hear much more of in the remainder of this book.

Throughout the '70s, the ARPA network grew. Its decentralised structure making expansion easy as it could accommodate different types of computers, as long as they could speak the standard packet-switching language. ARPA's original standard for communication was known as NCP short for 'Network Control Protocol', but this was soon superseded by the higher-level standard known as TCP/IP, which has survived until today.

TCP, or 'Transmission Control Protocol', converts messages into streams of packets at the source, then reassembles them back into messages at the destination. IP, or 'Internet Protocol', handles the addressing.

Over the years, ARPANET itself became a smaller and smaller part of the growing proliferation of other networked machines, but TCP/IP linked them all. As the '70s and '80s advanced, many different groups found themselves in possession of powerful computers. It was fairly easy to link these computers to the growing global network. As the use of TCP/IP, which was in the public-domain by that time, became more common, entire other networks were incorporated into the **Internet**.

In 1984 the National Science Foundation became involved and created the new NSFNET linking newer and faster supercomputers with bigger and faster links. Other US government agencies joined the bandwagon, including NASA, the National Institutes of Health and the Department of Energy.

ARPANET itself formally died in 1989, but its functions not only continued but were steadily improved. In Europe, major international 'backbone' networks started to provide connectivity to many millions of computers on a large number of other networks. Commercial network providers in both the US, Europe and Asia were beginning to offer Internet access and support on a competitive basis to any interested parties.

The extended use of the Internet cost the original founders little or nothing extra, since each new node was independent, and had to handle its own technical requirements and funding.

Today there are hundreds of thousands of nodes in the Internet, scattered throughout the world, with more coming on-line all the time and many millions of people using this often named 'Information Super Highway' every day.

Built to be indestructible and with no centralised control, it's no wonder the word 'anarchistic' is often bandied around when the Internet is discussed!

Why Use the Internet?

Now we know what the Internet is, what can we use it for? Five things, basically spring to mind; one is the reason for this book, and the other four are discussed briefly for completeness:

- sending and receiving e-mail messages, the subject of this book

- taking part in discussion groups

- accessing data stored on distant computers

- transferring data and program files from and to these distant computers

- browsing, or surfing the Net.

E-mail:

Electronic mail, has to be the main use of the Internet. It is very much faster that letter mail, which is known as 'snailmail' by regular e-mail users. It consists of electronic text, that is transmitted, sometimes in seconds, to anywhere else in the World that is connected to a main network. E-mail can also be used to send software and other types of files which are 'attached' to your message. As we shall see in later chapters, modern software makes this a very easy process.

Newsgroups:

Discussion groups, or 'newsgroups', are another feature of the Internet that are easily accessed with a good browser like the Microsoft Explorer. On the Internet they are generally known as USENET and consist of over 20,000 separate groups which let you freely participate in discussion on a vast number of subjects.

Long Distance Computing:

Using a program like Telnet you can maintain accounts on distant computers, run programs from them as if they were on your own PC, and generally make use of powerful supercomputers a continent away.

File Transfers:

There is a fantastic amount of free software available over the Internet, as well as a multitude of text and graphic files of almost any subject you care to mention.

File transfers carried out with a protocol known as FTP, allow Internet users to access remote machines and retrieve these for their own use. Many Internet computers allow anyone to access them anonymously, and to simply copy their public files, free of charge. With the right connections, entire books can be transferred in a matter of minutes.

Surfing the Net:

The World Wide Web, or Web as we shall call it, consists of client computers (yours and mine) and server computers which handle multimedia documents with 'hypertext' links built into them. Clicking the links on a page in a Web browser on your PC, brings documents located on a distant server to your screen, irrespective of the server's geographic location. Documents may contain text, images, sounds, movies, or a combination of these, in other words - multimedia.

Up until recently all of these activities required very expensive computing facilities and a large measure of computer literacy. Times have changed, however, and it is now possible to fairly easily and cheaply install a modem in your PC, connect to the Internet and with a World Wide Web browser, like Netscape, or Microsoft Explorer, carry them out with very little technical knowledge.

2. THE BASIC REQUIREMENTS

To be able to use the Internet's e-mail facilities you need a few basic items.

Computer Hardware

First, you obviously need a computer! We have written this book with the current most common combination in mind - a PC running under Windows 95. But most of the e-mail programs described have versions for other types of computers using other operating systems. Most of our chapters will be equally useful if you use an older version of Windows, a Macintosh, or even dare we say it, Unix.

The minimum hardware requirements to run Windows 95, are a 486, or higher, PC with 4 MB of RAM (but at least 8 and preferably 16 MB are recommended), a VGA Display (SVGA with 256 colours or higher is recommended), and as much hard disc space as you can get your hands on.

You also need a connection to the Internet, via a Modem, Ethernet Card, or ISDN direct digital phone line. A digital ISDN line is faster than a modem connection, but is considerably more expensive, at the moment. Unless you are lucky enough to have a PC which is connected to a Local Area Network which has Internet access, you will need a modem to be able to communicate with the rest of the world. This is a device that converts data so that it can be transmitted over the analogue telephone system.

A Connection to the Internet

If your PC at work is networked and has Internet access you can ignore this section. If not, you will need to find, and subscribe to, a suitable Internet provider.

When we went to press, there were about 50 such providers in the UK. They can be listed on the Web by accessing the following address:

http://thelist.iworld.com/

and selecting the United Kingdom. Alternatively you could try your telephone directory, or possibly adverts in the computer section of your local paper.

Two of the e-mail packages we describe later are built into Web browsers, so what you are ideally looking for is **full dial-up SLIP or PPP connection with unlimited WWW access to the Internet**, and hopefully, this should be possible by dialling a local number to your provider's access point. (SLIP and PPP are only two communication standards that you need to have, but do not need to understand).

The local call access will mean your phone bills should not be excessive, especially if you do your Web browsing in off-peak times. The unlimited access means you will not pay any extra to your Internet Provider no matter how many hours you spend glued to your PC. Such a service will probably cost in the order of £30 to set up and about £150 per year thereafter, plus the ubiquitous VAT of course.

The other two e-mail packages described do not require full WWW access. You may be able to negotiate e-mail only facilities from your provider and save some money. The choice is yours.

If you need to purchase and install a modem, your Internet Provider will probably be able to provide one, along with all the necessary cables, connections, software, help and back up that is bound to be required.

From now on in this book, we assume that you have an active connection to the Internet. Trouble shooting this is not within our remit!

E-mail Software

Once you have your computer set up and connected to the Internet all you need to handle your e-mail is a suitable software program. There are many available and some can cost you considerable sums of money. We describe four e-mail programs in the chapters that follow, all of which are freely available and can be downloaded from the Internet. There are many more, but we feel that these four contain, between them, all the facilities you could possibly need.

In fact two of them are built into the main Web browsers, Netscape and Microsoft Explorer. If you use either of these browsers you will already have their e-mail facilities built in. The other two are the very commonly used programs, Eudora and Pegasus. The order of chapters that follows is in no way meant to rank these packages, but after spending time with all of them we must admit to a preference for Pegasus.

We suggest you read about each package and, if it sounds right for you, download it and try it out. You can always remove it from your system if you don't like it.

E-mail Addresses

Every e-mail user must have a unique address so that messages can be correctly routed to them. An e-mail address usually has two main parts, which are separated with the '@' character, and usually contain at least one dot (the '.' character). The following is a typical, if short, example.

aperson@organisation.co.uk

The part before the @ is the user name which identifies him, or her, at the mailbox. This user name is usually made up from the name and initials of the user, and must be unique on the mailbox server.

After the @ comes the domain name, which identifies the computer where the person has a mailbox and is usually the name of a company, a university, or other organisation. There is a central register of these domain names, as each must be unique worldwide. When you set up your account, you can sometimes get your service provider to customise a domain name for you, at a price, of course. Otherwise you will probably use the domain name of the service provider itself.

Next, there's a '.' or dot, followed by two, or three, letters that indicate the type of domain it is. In our example above this is **.co** which means the host is a business or commercial enterprise, located in the United Kingdom (**.uk**). In the USA this would be **.com** instead, but not followed by a country identifier. A host name ending with **.edu** means the host is a US university or educational facility. A UK university would be **.ac.uk**. A **.org** indicates the host is a US non-commercial organisation.

Some of the more common extensions you might encounter are:

edu	Educational sites in the US
com	Commercial sites in the US
gov	Government sites in the US
net	Network administrative organisations
mil	Military sites in the US
org	Organisations in the US that don't fit into other categories
fr	France
ca	Canada
uk	United Kingdom

Once you get used to these parts of addresses they begin to make more sense. For example, the writer's e-mail address is

poliver@csm.ex.ac.uk

This reads quite easily as:

P. Oliver located at Camborne School of Mines, part of the University of Exeter, which is an academic institution in the UK.

So if you know where somebody works you can even make an attempt to guess his, or her, e-mail address. A home address obtained through a commercial Internet provider would not be very easy though!

Finding an E-mail Address:

There are several good e-mail address directory sites available over the World Wide Web. One of them, the FOUR11 White Page Directory can be accessed with the following URL address:

www.four11.com

The search screen that opens is shown here.

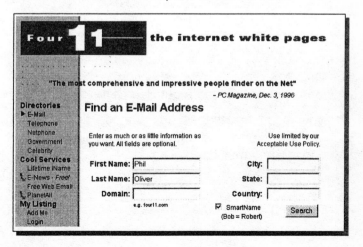

We did not really expect to get a positive search result, but were surprised to find over 20 Phil Olivers, and near phonetic matches, in the directory.

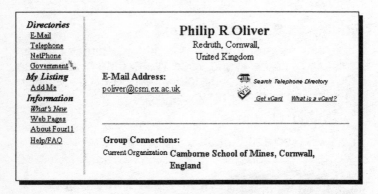

Clicking on the bottom one of those listed above gave the following quite complete personal details.

If you don't find your details here, you can click the <u>Add Me</u> link to remedy the situation. These e-mail directories are getting more detailed all the time.

If you send messages to one of the Internet Newsgroups, your e-mail address is often automatically added to these e-mail directories.

The E-mail Message

Before we get started with the e-mail programs perhaps a few words are in order about the actual content of electronic messages.

Message Headers:

Most people will have used memos that have a series of headers at the beginning of the message text. They may look something like the following:

To: Noel Kantaris
From: Phil Oliver
Subject: Microsoft Office 97
Date: 27 March 1997

E-mails have headers that are very similar and are essential for us so that we can see who a message is meant for, what it's about, who sent it, and when. They have a more important use though, because as long as headers are consistently formatted, any e-mail program can easily sort out and present the messages received on a computer. It is this which allows users with different e-mail packages, in different types of computers, to send each other electronic messages.

The Body of the Message:

Usually the body makes up the bulk of an e-mail message and looks very similar to any other word processed letter. Older e-mail programs were often limited to handling text in the ASCII character set, but the current generation allow elaborately formatted text and graphics, sound, and even multimedia video clips.

The MIME Protocol:

The use of multimedia was not possible with the original Simple Mail Transfer Protocol (SMTP - a very common e-mail protocol), so a new protocol, called

MIME (Multi-purpose Internet Mail Extension) was developed, which allows you to include almost anything in an e-mail message.

As long as you both have MIME-enabled e-mail programs you can exchange any kind of multimedia file by simply appending it to your message. All of the e-mail programs described in this book are MIME-enabled, but you should check to make sure that the recipient also has MIME, before sending them non-text attachments.

3. PEGASUS MAIL

Pegasus Mail is an e-mail program we have only recently started using. But we are so impressed with the package and its wealth of features, that we have no hesitation in recommending it. It is provided by its author free of charge "as a service to the  broader community of people seeking to benefit from electronic mail". You can use Pegasus Mail on as many systems as you wish without cost or obligation. An optional manual can be purchased, but with our few pages and the built in Help system we don't think you will need one, unless of course, you want to show your appreciation to the author.

Pegasus Features

At the time of writing, WinPMail v2.5 was the latest 32 Bit release of Pegasus Mail for Windows NT and Windows 95. Some of its features include:

- A **spellchecker**, with an Autocheck option to invoke it automatically when a message is sent.

- An **Autosave** option to periodically save messages, in case of a system crash.

- **Multiple Identities** can be set up in the same mailbox.

- The ability to **drag and drop** messages between folders.

- If you receive **HTML mail** messages, from Netscape for example, Pegasus offers to run your Web browser to display them.

- Up to 64 **attachments** per message.

- **Multiple signatures** - you can define up to nine different signature sets.

- The ability to toggle between **regular and monospaced font** views in the message editor. This is useful for aligning columns or tables.

- **Global Folder Search** lets you search for words and phrases across all your folders.

- Web links - **URLs** - are highlighted in a message, double-clicking them will activate your web browser.

- **Long filename support** for Windows 95 and Windows NT.

- You can create a **business card** with your address and contact details.

- Automatically keeps **copies** of all your outgoing mail.

- **Message encryption** using a very secure algorithm, with the ability to use encryptors developed by third parties.

- A **Glossary** feature speeds up entry of common text and phrases.

- **Mail filtering** automates your mail processing.

- Extensive **address book** features with aliasing.

- **Distribution lists** allow mailing to hundreds or thousands of users.

- Extremely comprehensive context-sensitive on-line **Help** system.

- Comprehensive support for the **Internet MIME** multimedia messaging standard.

- Public **noticeboard/discussion** group features.

- **Hierarchical folders** with mail folders within mail folders for optimum organisation of mail.

- You can **access** an unlimited number of POP3 mailboxes at an unlimited number of sites.

- An **extensions** feature allows developers to create their own extra functions that look and behave just like part of the Pegasus program.

- A **Selective download** feature which lets you retrieve message headers and their sizes from your mailbox, and then allows you to retrieve or delete the messages from the mailbox.

Getting the Software

After reading that list of features you should be wanting to know how to get your copy of Pegasus. Some of the officially-maintained sources are:

1. Via anonymous FTP on the Internet:

   ftp.let.rug.nl, in the /pmail folder

2. Using your Web Browser on the Internet:

   http://www.let.rug.nl/pegasus

3. On CompuServe:

   Usually in the NOVUSER area. Doing a keyword search on the word 'Pegasus' will find it for you.

4. By mail:

   You can also obtain Pegasus Mail by sending a self-addressed unstamped envelope and US$10 or equivalent in cash to cover postage and the cost of the discs. Send to the author:

   Pegasus Mail, c/o David Harris
   P.O. Box 5451,
   Dunedin,
   New Zealand.

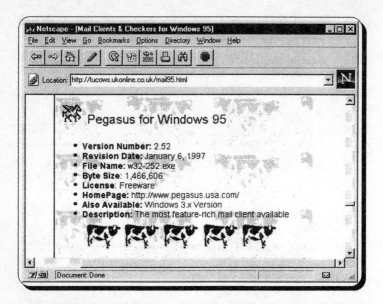

We found our version at one of our favourite sources of Internet software, a site called Tucows, which has a UK mirror site, as shown above.

To download the program file, first access the above site in your Web browser by typing the URL address shown in the **Location:** text box. Then, simply clicking the Pegasus for Windows 95 link, and giving a file saving location when asked, will start the transfer process. It is always a good idea to have a temporary storage area on your hard disc for these occasions. Ours is a directory, or folder, called *temp*.

Installing Pegasus

W32-252.exe

Double-clicking the downloaded program file - W32-252.EXE - in a Windows 95 Explorer window, will start installing the program. This self-extracts the files and loads a Set-up Wizard which steps you easily through the whole installation.

18

Starting Pegasus

When you open your Windows 95 START menu you will find a new group in the **Programs** section, as

shown here. To start the program, click the **Pegasus Mail for Win32** option. At this stage, however, we suggest you choose **Getting Started with Pegasus Mail** and spend a few minutes with the very good tutorial. The Help facilities with this package are really excellent.

Setting Up Mailboxes

The first time you open Pegasus you have to set up your mailbox configuration from the window below. These procedures are very self explanatory, but if you are installing onto an existing network and you have problems with the best settings, we suggest you get some help from your Network Administrator.

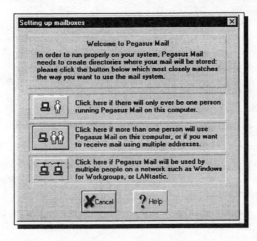

Single User Configuration:

 If you have a single e-mail address and will be the only person running Pegasus on your computer, click the single user button and accept the mail folder, or directory, name suggested. This is where your mail-related files will be stored by the program.

Multi-user Configuration:

 Click this button if you want more than one person to use Pegasus Mail on this computer, each with their own mailbox and preference files. In multi-user mode, Pegasus will prompt for a username when it is run. You can also use this option if you send and receive mail using more than one e-mail address, by creating a separate user account for each address.

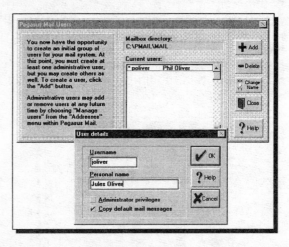

With this option, the next window to open lets you enter brief details of the Mail Users, as shown above. Click the **Add** button and enter the **Username** and **Personal name** of everyone who will have access to e-mail on the PC. Click the **Help** button if you want more detail at any stage.

When you set up with more than one user the program asks for the User name every time it is started up, as shown here.

Connecting to Your Server

Before you can use Pegasus to send, or receive, mail you have to tell the program how to connect to your server's facilities. You can do this in two ways. By completing your personal e-mail connection details in the Wizard, which opens when you first attempt to use the program. The other way is to use the options box, shown below, which is opened when the **Tools**, **Options**, menu command is actioned from the main Pegasus window, and the **Network configuration** category is clicked.

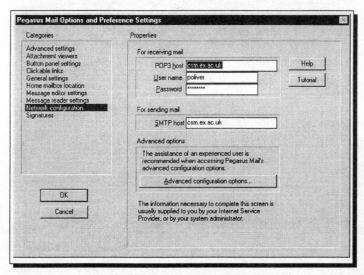

To complete the details in this box you may need to ask your Internet service provider or system administrator for your details. The ones shown here will obviously only work for the writer.

You enter the address of your POP3 server in the **POP3 host** field; your e-mail name (only the part that precedes the @ sign in your e-mail address) into the **User name** text field, and the address of your SMTP server in the **SMTP host** field. The password to enter, in the **Password** field, is the one to open the mailbox on your server. Details of all these should have been given to you by your Internet service provider or system administrator when you opened your 'service account'. When you have finished, press **OK** to close the box and save your changes.

The first time Pegasus mail opened for us, four messages, which had been saved on our hard disc during the installation, were displayed in the New mail folder, as shown below.

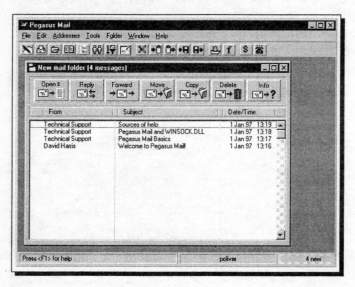

To read these messages in the Reader window, select the first one in the list and either double-click it, or click the **Open** icon, shown here. When you have read each message click the **Next** icon and work your way through all four. The last one, shown below, is a 'personal' message from author of Pegasus.

To check your own mail, click the **Read new mail** icon, shown below, or use the **File**, **Read new mail** menu

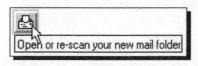 command, or use the <Ctrl+W> quick key combination. All of these will download any new messages from your mailbox to your hard disc. You can then read and process your mail at your leisure without necessarily being still connected to the Internet.

23

With the default set-up, Pegasus will only check your mailbox when you ask it to. You can force it to check your mail at regular intervals in the **Tools**, **Options**, **Network configuration**, **Advanced configuration options** settings sheet. Setting the **Check for new POP3 mail ...** option, as shown below, will make the program check your mail box when it starts and at one minute intervals while it is open.

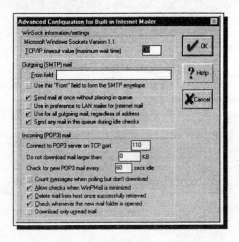

Before making any changes in one of these configuration sheets we strongly recommend that you click its **Help** button and study the options available.

A Trial Run

Before explaining in more detail the main features of Pegasus Mail we will step through the procedure of sending a very simple e-mail message. The best way to test out any unfamiliar e-mail features is to send a test message to your own e-mail address. This saves wasting somebody else's time, and the message can be very quickly checked to see the results.

 Click the **New message** icon, to open the Message editor window, shown on the facing page.

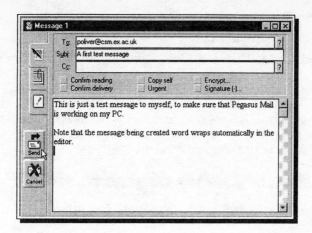

Type your own e-mail address in the **To:** field, and a title for the message in the **Subj:** field. The text in this

subject field will form a header for the message when it is received, so it helps to show in a few words what the message is about. Type your message and when you are happy with it, click the **Send** icon.

By default, outgoing messages are stored in a queue, and are only sent when you action the **File**, **Send all queued mail** command. If you look on the Advanced Configuration settings sheet you will see that ours is set to **Send mail at once without placing in queue**. When Pegasus next checks for mail, it will find the message and download it into the New mail folder, as shown below, for you to open and read.

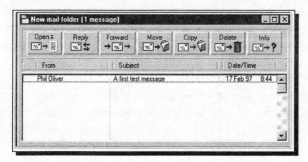

The Main Window

Pegasus Mail uses a Main window, which stays open all the time, and several others, which depend on the action being performed. The three most important of these are the Folder window, which lists the messages in the currently selected folder; the Reader window for reading your mail; and the Message window, to compose your outgoing mail messages.

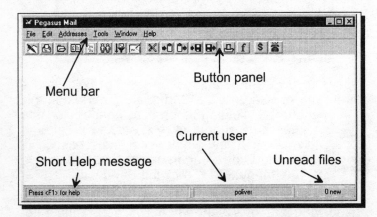

The Main window consists of the program menu bar and a toolbar, or 'button panel', with the default display shown in our example above. You can choose different Button panel layouts from the **Tools**, **Options**, **Button panel** settings sheet, but we will let you try these out for yourself.

The button panel and menu bar in the Main window are always available while Pegasus is active. When you explore the different menu options note the short Help message on the bottom Status bar that refers to the currently selected menu option.

When a Message, Folder or Reader window is active their own icons are then available, and an extra menu option is also added to the menu bar, located between **Tools** and **Window** .

The Button Panel:

The Button panel on the Main window is a set of tools which provides access to the most commonly-used parts of the program at the click of a button. Depending on your settings the Button panel can appear as either a fixed toolbar beneath the main menu, or as a small floating window.

When the Button panel is active as a toolbar, the main program buttons have the following functions:

 Compose a new message

 Read new mail

 Open/manage mail folders

 Open/manage address books

 Open/manage distribution lists

 Open the local user list

 New mail filtering rules

 Use the noticeboard system

 Cut selection to the clipboard

 Copy selection to the clipboard

Paste the contents of the clipboard

Save or write to disc

Retrieve or import from disc

Print

Select font

Order Pegasus manuals

Compose a telephone message

The following three buttons will only appear if the built-in TCP/IP mail subsystem using WINSOCK.DLL is available for use:

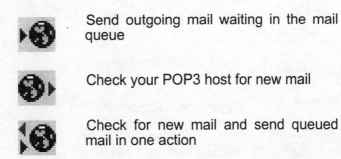

Send outgoing mail waiting in the mail queue

Check your POP3 host for new mail

Check for new mail and send queued mail in one action

When the Button panel is active as a floating window there is no main toolbar, only five bigger buttons with the following functions:

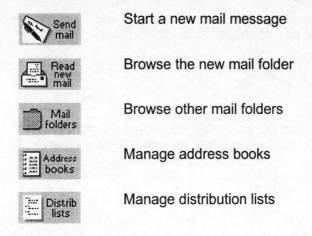

Start a new mail message

Browse the new mail folder

Browse other mail folders

Manage address books

Manage distribution lists

Organising Your Mail in Folders

As we have already seen with Pegasus, when you first receive a new e-mail message it is listed in the New Mail folder. When you have read it a small tick

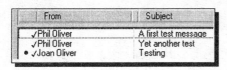

appears in the status area at the left end of the line entry, as shown here. If you send a reply to the message a blue dot is also placed in this area.

As soon as you close the New Mail folder all the files that have been read are moved to the Main folder. This is quite a good feature as whenever you look in the New mail window you are not faced with lots of already read messages that are awaiting filing, as with most other e-mail programs. The Main folder is the holding area. It will not be long, though, before you will have to 'file' the messages that are worth keeping so that you can more easily find them.

The easiest way of doing this is to build a hierarchical structure of storage folders.

To do this, first click the Folders icon on the Button panel and double-click the Main folder item.

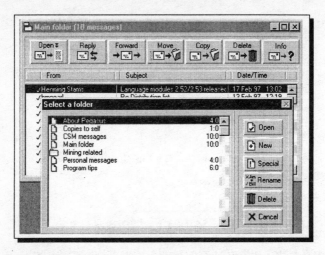

This will open the Main folder, which has a series of icons that let you manipulate your messages. Choose a message that you want to file and click the
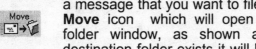
Move icon which will open the Select a folder window, as shown above. If the destination folder exists it will be listed here, in which case selecting it and clicking the **Open** icon will move the message there. If it does not exist, click the **New** icon, and enter a **Long name for..** the new folder. Make sure the **Message folder** option is selected and then click **OK**. The new folder will be created and the message will be moved to it. If you want to create sub-folders, within other folders, you must first create a **Filing tray**, double-click it to open it, and then create the new sub-folders within it.

Once your folder structure is created you can easily drag messages (with the left mouse button depressed) between open windows to move them. Copy them by dragging with the <Alt> key depressed as well. To select more than one message in a list, hold down the <Ctrl> key and click each one in turn.

The Folder Menu:

When a folder window is active the menu bar offers **Folder** related options, as shown here. This includes options to sort the message list, to copy a message to file, to colour a message header in the folder list, to set some of your folders as Quick folders that you can rapidly move and copy files to, to add annotations to a message, and to change the viewing font.

Deleting Messages:

To delete a message in a Folder window, first select it and then either press the <Del> key, or click the **Delete** icon. By default with Pegasus, deleted messages are removed from your PC immediately. This can be a little dangerous at first, when you are learning to move your messages around. We suggest you select the **Preserve deleted messages until exit** option in the **Tools**, **Options**, **General settings** sheet. Your deleted messages will then be placed in the temporary Deleted messages folder, which will itself be deleted, with its contents, when you close the program.

Keeping Message Copies:

Unlike most e-mail programs, Pegasus does not automatically keep a copy of all the messages you send. If you want to do this, check the **Copy self** box in the Message editing window. A copy of your message will be placed in a folder called Copies to self. Pegasus will remember this setting from message to message and between sessions; they call this a 'sticky setting'.

31

The Reader Window

If you double-click a message in a Folder window list
the Reader window is opened, as shown below.

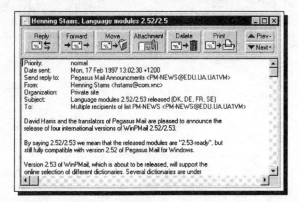

This is the window you read your mail in. It has its own
Reader menu options and icon set, which let you
rapidly process and move between the messages in a
folder. The **Move** and **Delete** options we have met
before, but some of the others are new.

Replying to a Message:

When you want to reply to an e-mail
message, Pegasus Mail makes it very easy
to do. Simply click the **Reply** icon, accept the

Reply options shown here,
and the reply address and
subject fields are both
automatically added for
you in a new Message
window. With these
settings, the original
message is quoted in the
editing area for you to alter
as required.

Using Quoted Text:

It is almost an e-mail standard now to place the '>' character at the beginning of every line of quoted text in a message. Pegasus can do this automatically.

You should not, however, leave all of the original message, including all its headers, in your reply. This is not good practice and rapidly makes new messages very large and time consuming to download. You should edit the quoted text, so that it is obvious what you are referring to. Usually one or two lines is enough.

Forwarding a Message:

If you want to send a message on to someone else, click the **Forward** icon and complete the message box shown below. There is an interesting feature in this box. If you click the '?' button to the right of the text field, a list of your most recently used e-mail addresses is opened up. Selecting one of these saves you

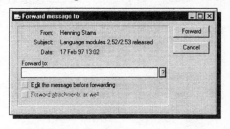

the bother of typing it in. The **Edit the message before forwarding** option lets you do just that.

Viewing File Attachments:

Until fairly recently, e-mail was good only for short text notes. You couldn't send attachments like formatted document or graphic files with your messages. That has now changed with the advent of MIME, which stands for Multipurpose Internet Mail Extension. With Pegasus you can send and receive formatted documents, photos, sound and video files as attachments to your main e-mail message.

If a message has an attachment, a black rectangular mark is shown in its status area, as shown above. When you open such a message, the **Reader** window looks a little different, and gives you the choice of which part of the message you want to look at.

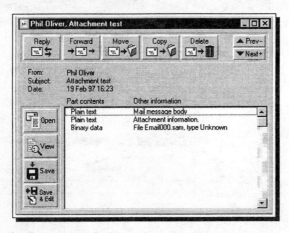

In our example above, an Ami Pro file with a '.SAM' extension, was attached to the message. If you select the attachment item in the list (the bottom one in ours above), and try to **Open** such a Binary attachment, you will be politely told to do something else! The editor cannot read unknown binary files, only text files.

To display the attachment, click the **View** icon, and the host program, in this case the Ami Pro word processor, is started, with the attachment file already loaded.

To save an attachment, click the **Save** icon and give the saving location when asked. The **Save & Edit** option combines the last two, the attached file is saved on your hard disc and then opened for you to work on.

34

Printing a Message:

We can still remember the concept of a 'paperless office', but however sophisticated electronic messaging becomes there is still the need for some hard copy on paper. Clicking the **Print** icon starts the process and opens the Print mail message(s) dialogue box shown here.

This lets you choose and **Setup** your **Printer**, set the paper margins and printing **Font** and gives you four options for printing the message headers. Being a Windows program you don't need to worry at all about installing your printer for Pegasus. That is all done centrally for all Windows programs.

Reading HTML Messages:

Some e-mail messages you receive may have been created for viewing in a Web browser, such as Microsoft Explorer. They are text files written in HTML, which stands for HyperText Markup Language. When you attempt to open one of these files, you will be asked if you want your Web browser to open with the message loaded, or if you want to view the message text in a Pegasus Reader window.

URL Links in a Message:

Pegasus Mail can detect hypertext links, or URLs (Uniform Resource Locators), in a message. When it finds one, it highlights it by displaying it in underlined green text. Double-clicking on the link will load your browser and open the linked Web page.

The Message Window

We briefly looked into the Message window earlier in the chapter. This is the window, shown below, that you use to create any messages you want to send electronically from Pegasus.

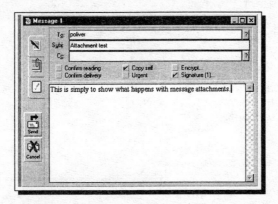

 As we saw, this window can be opened by using the **New message** toolbar icon, as well as the **File, New Message** menu command, or the <Ctrl+N> keyboard shortcut from the Main Pegasus window.

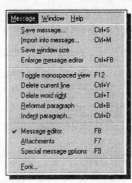

A Message window has its own set of icons, and a **Message** menu option, as shown here, is placed on the menu bar. Both of which let you rapidly prepare and send your new e-mail messages.

The Message window has three main views which are controlled by the tabbed icons on the left hand side. When opened it shows the editing area, as in our example above. This is where you enter the message header details and the text body of the message.

Ticking any of the six option boxes lets you:

- Confirm that the message has been delivered.

- Confirm that it has been read. This option is only really of use on an internal network where the recipient also uses Pegasus.

- Place a copy of the message sent in the Copy to self folder on your hard disc.

- Mark a message as urgent.

- Encrypt, or code, the message, for added security.

- Automatically add your signature to the bottom of the message.

Checking Your Spelling:

This is the only free e-mail program we have used with a fully fledged spell checker built in. How many messages have you sent out without reading first, only to be horrified with your text when it is quoted back to you in a reply!

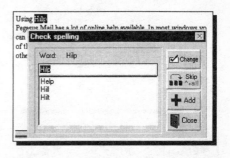

With Pegasus this need never happen again. To check the spelling of your message, action the **Tools**, **Check spelling** menu command, or the <Ctrl+K> quick key combination. If a mistake is found, the suspect word is highlighted in the message and the Check spelling window is opened as shown above. You can correct the word in the text box provided, or select the correct one from the offered list, and click the **Change** icon to make the correction. If you are happy with the original word click the **Skip** button. If you do not want Pegasus to query the word in the future click the **Add** button, and it will be added to the dictionary. The **Close** button is self explanatory.

If you don't want to bother with doing this manually, you can select to **Automatically check spelling before sending message** in the **Tools**, **Options**, **Message editor settings** sheet.

Adding Attachments

 If you want to send a file as an attachment to your main e-mail message you simply click the **Attachment** tab button and select the file to attach, as shown below.

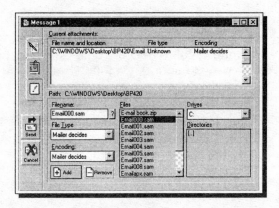

Locate the file, or files, to attach in the **Drives**, **Directories**, and **Files** list boxes, and with the correct file shown in the **Filename** box, click the **Add** button.

 Clicking the third tab button in the Message window opens a set of **Advanced addressing and formatting options**, which allow you to customise your message even further.

Sending an E-mail

Send

When you have filled in the address fields, typed and formatted the body of your message, added any attachments, and maybe placed a signature as described next, you simply click the **Send** Toolbar button, shown here, to start the transmission process. What happens to the message next depends on your option settings.

If you want to hold the message and send it later, maybe with several others to save on your telephone bill, make sure the **Send mail at once without placing in queue** option is not selected in the **Tools**, **Options**, **Network configuration**, **Advanced configuration options** settings sheet. In this case, clicking the above **Send** Toolbar icon places the message in the 'queue'.

When you are ready to send your held messages you click the **Check and send** Toolbar icon on the Main window, or use the **File**, **Check and send mail** menu command.

When the **Send mail at once without placing in queue** option is selected, your messages will be sent on their way as soon as you click the **Send** button. This option is best used if you have a permanent connection to the Internet, or your e-mail is being sent over an internal network, or Intranet.

Your Own Signature

A signature is text that Pegasus automatically adds to the end of your messages when they are sent. It usually contains your name, address and telephone and fax numbers, although some people place quotations as well, or really go overboard with text graphics.

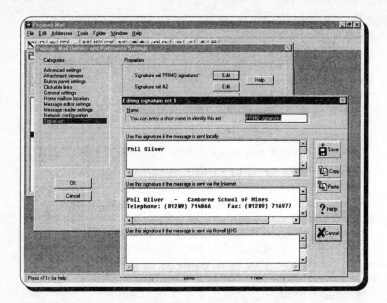

You create a signature, or set of signatures, in the **Tools**, **Options**, **Signatures** setting sheets, as shown above. Pegasus supports nine different signatures sets that you can select for any message, though most people will only need one. Clicking the **Edit** button against a set shows that each one can have three signatures - one for mail sent 'in house', one that will be attached to Internet mail, and a third for messages sent by Novell MHS, (Novell's messaging system).

Enter a **Name** for the set and then the text for the different options. The **Copy** and **Paste** icons can cut down on keyboard use! When you are happy with your signatures click the **Save** button, followed by **OK**.

To select a signature set for your mail message, click the **Signature** check box in the Message editor window, which opens the dialogue box shown here.

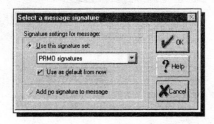

This lets you select which signature set to use. Check the **Use as default from now** option if you always want to use that set.

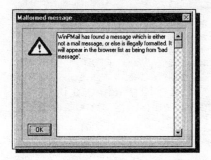

A word of warning - do not select to attach a signature set to your message unless you have actually created it. Pegasus can get a little upset if you do and present the message box shown here.

Using Address Books

E-mail addresses are often quite complicated and not easy to remember at all. With Pegasus there is a very useful Address Book facility built in, which lets you store your e-mail addresses in folders. Clicking the **Address book** icon on the Main window toolbar lets you select which address book to use.

To create a new one, click the **New** button and type its name in the **Long name for item** field shown below.

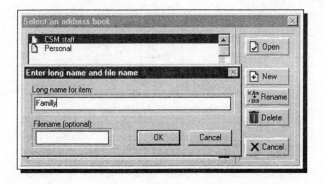

It is very easy to change an address book name, maybe because you did not spell it correctly! The

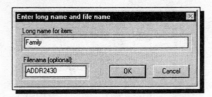

Rename icon opens the same box so that you can try again. If you leave the **Filename (optional)** field empty, as we did, Pegasus names the address book file and saves it in the Mail folder with a '.pmr' extension.

You open an address book by double-clicking its name in the list, or by selecting it and pressing the **Open** icon. The **Add** icon opens the **Edit address book entry** dialogue box, shown below. The **Edit** icon lets you change the details of an individual entry later on.

You must put entries in the **Name (alias)**, **Key**, and **E-mail address** fields, the others are optional. We could not get the **Set picture** option to work, but we did not try very hard.

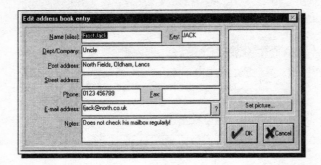

We will leave it to you to find your way round this very useful facility. The Help system covers it quite well in the section opened with the commands, **Help**, **Help index**, **Address books**.

To send a new message to anyone listed, simply double-click their entry in an address book. A Message window will be opened with their destination address already entered.

To send, or copy, the same message to several listed people, open a Message window and make the **To:** field active to send, or the **Cc:** field active to copy. Then, in your address books, select each person in turn and click the **Paste** button on the Address book window. Any highlighted addresses will be copied into the active field in the message you are editing.

You can also drag address entries from an address book to an open destination field, or if you want, to other open Windows applications.

Distribution Lists

A Pegasus message address field can only hold up to 180 characters, so if you need to send a message to more addresses than will fit in this space, or you have lists of users to whom you mail regularly, you will need to create distribution lists.

The procedure for this is similar to that for address books, and is covered very well in the Pegasus Help system. To access it, use the **Help**, **Help index**, **Distribution lists** menu commands.

We must stress that it is essential you read the section on Distribution List Options, which we copy on the next page, when setting up. The contents of the **To: field** are critical to distribution list operation.

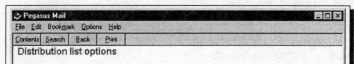

Distribution list options

There are several ways you can control and customize the operation of your distribution lists.

To field: Entering an address in this field will force Pegasus Mail to suppress the listing of all the recipients' addresseses in the To: field when you use the list. Instead of showing every member of the list, the To: field will contain only what you enter here. Because of the way Internet mail works, you cannot simply enter any piece of text in this field -- you must enter something which can be legally processed as if it were an address. We recommend that you use the following format to create the contents of this field:

"*(descriptive text)*" <*(your own address)*>

Replace *(descriptive text)* with a meaningful name for the mailing list, and put your own address where it says *(your own address)*. Recipients will almost always see the descriptive text instead of your address so it will not seem as strange as it sounds. The quote characters around *(descriptive text)* and the angle bracket characters around *(your own address)* are vitally important and must be included exactly as shown. It is not possible to suppress the recipient list for MHS mail and this field will be ignored for MHS messages.

Reply to: If you want to direct replies to list mailings to a particular address, enter it here. A reply-to field you set in the list will override any in the message.

Confirm reading, confirm delivery, urgent, no signature: These controls duplicate the same features in the message editor. If you set them for the distribution list they will override the values you use when you compose the message.

Filtering Your Incoming Mail

If you are ever in the situation of receiving e-mail messages from a regular source that you do not want to hear from, you can filter your incoming messages with Pegasus. Unwanted ones can be deleted without you even having to bother with them. Filtering is also useful for sorting incoming messages and automatically routing them to their correct folders.

 Clicking the **Filtering rules** icon in the Main window opens the Rules for new mail window shown in our screen dump on the facing page. This lists all the rules that have been set, and allows you to **Erase**, or **Edit** them, or to **Add** new ones.

44

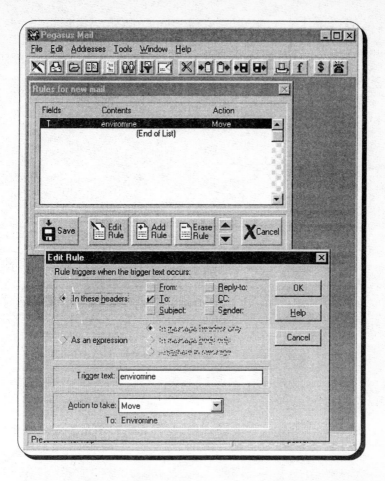

In our example we have set up one simple filter rule that looks for the word 'enviromine' in the **To:** field of all our new messages as they are downloaded from the server mailbox. (These are received from a mailing list we belong to). When such a message is found, it is automatically moved to the Enviromine mail folder.

If you look in the **Action to take** drop-down list, you will find 18 options you can choose, ranging from deleting the message to playing a sound!

You can set multiple rules for incoming messages, but if an incoming message matches more than one rule, then it is treated according to the first rule it matches in your list.

We will leave it to you to delve deeper into this excellent facility on your own.

* * * * * * * *

The Pegasus e-mail program contains more facilities than we have been able to cover here. We hope you enjoy finding some of them. Don't forget the Help system, it is always there.

4. NETSCAPE MAIL

Netscape 3 also has a very powerful mail facility built into their Navigator browser, which makes it very easy for you to send and receive e-mail.

Getting the Netscape Browser

If you are actually connected to the Internet you can download Netscape software and evaluate it for free. All Netscape products, that are available for electronic download, are free to all students and staff of educational institutions, and to charitable non-profit organisations and public libraries. These users are not, however, entitled to technical support. Other users are supposed to pay for the software after a 90 day evaluation period. But how many do, we've no idea!

If you are not yet connected, you have more of a problem getting the software. The best thing would be to get yourself on line and connected to the Internet, as briefly described in Chapter 2, and using the browser supplied by your Internet provider, download what you want from the Netscape Web pages.

Alternatively you could purchase a packaged hard copy of your Navigator for about £30, with the added advantage that you would then get a manual and be entitled to technical support from Netscape.

We will outline the procedure for downloading Netscape Navigator version 3.1 for Windows 95. First you must access the Netscape Web page, shown on the next page, by entering the following URL address.

http://home.netscape.com/comprod/mirror/client_download.html

As things have a habit of changing very rapidly on the Web, if this does not work by the time you read this, you may have to improvise a little. In this case go to Netscape's home page at:

http://home.netscape.com/

and follow the hypertext links for downloading software.

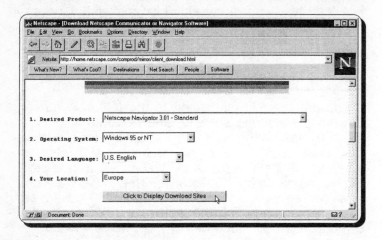

To complete the entries in the form, open the drop-down lists by clicking the arrow on their right end and make your selection from the list. This is a quick way to ensure that you actually download a version of Netscape that is correct for your system.

Next press the **Click to Display Download Sites** button to open a page of sites that can provide the software. You should select the site which is nearest to you to speed up the transfer process. In the UK this would probably be one of the following:

Download: HENSA/micros at Lancaster University, UK
Download: SunSITE UK at Imperial College, London, UK
Download: University of Edinburgh, UK

Clicking an entry, and giving a file saving location when asked, will start the transfer process. It is always a good idea to have a temporary storage area on your hard disc for these occasions. Ours is a directory, or folder, called *temp*.

If you selected a version of Netscape Navigator 3.1 for Windows 95 the file N32E31.EXE, or one with a name very much like it, should eventually arrive in your temporary directory.

If you have trouble downloading with your current browser, you could also try getting the file directly from one of the FTP servers by clicking the link **FTP Servers** on the **Download Netscape Navigator Software** page, and then following the on-screen instructions.

Installing Netscape

From a Windows 95 Explorer window double-clicking the downloaded .EXE program file will start the installation procedure. This loads the InstallShield Wizard which steps you easily through the whole procedure.

When you have finished and finally return to the Windows 95 desktop you will find that a new Shortcut icon has been placed on it, as shown here. Double-clicking on this icon will start the Netscape Navigator.

Using Netscape Mail

Before you can use your Navigator to send, or receive, mail you have to tell the program how to connect to your server's facilities. You do this in the preference box, shown on the next page, which is opened when the **Options**, **Mail and News Preferences** menu command is actioned, and the **Servers** tab is clicked.

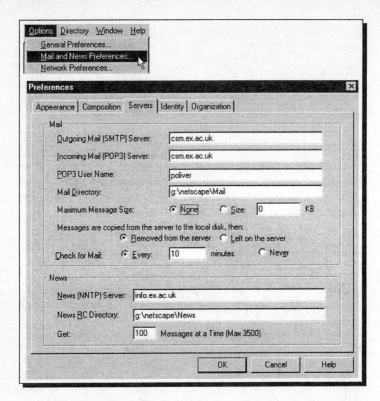

To complete the first two options in this box you may need to ask your Internet service provider, or system administrator, for your details. The ones above will obviously only work for the writer, so don't try them!

You type your e-mail name (only the part that precedes the @ sign in your e-mail address) into the **POP3 User Name** text field. Without this, Netscape will not know which mailbox to look in! The other options will probably not need any changes.

Before you leave the Preferences section, click the **Identity** tab and enter your own details, not ours as shown on the next page. These will identify you on any e-mail messages you send. Press the **Help** button if you need to know more.

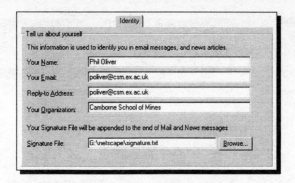

We will cover the **Signature File** option later in the chapter. When you have finished press **OK** to close each box and save your changes.

Opening the Mail Window

There are two ways to open the Mail window:

- Use the **Window**, **Netscape Mail** command.

- Click the mail icon, which shows as an envelope at the right end of the status bar.

As long as your Internet connection is active, they both ask for your password, as shown here. The password to enter is the one to open the mailbox on your server.

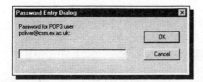

Details of this should have been given to you by your Internet provider or system administrator when you opened your 'service account'.

Once Netscape accepts your password it will open the Mail window and download any new messages from your mailbox to the Mail folder on your hard disc (specified in the **Mail Directory** field of the Servers Preferences dialogue box).

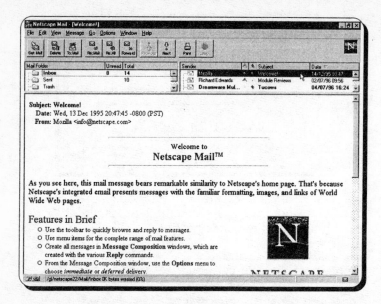

You can then read and process your mail at your leisure without necessarily being still connected to the Internet.

Netscape will automatically check your mailbox at regular intervals for new mail, but to retrieve any new messages in the future, click the mail icon. This icon changes to show if you have any new messages in the mailbox, as follows:

 A question mark next to the envelope means that Netscape cannot automatically check the status of the mail server. This appears before you've opened the Mail window or supplied your password.

 The envelope alone indicates there are no new messages for you.

 An exclamation mark next to the envelope indicates that new messages are waiting. Clicking the icon will retrieve them for you.

A Trial Run

Before explaining in more detail the features of Netscape Mail, we will step through the procedure of sending a very simple e-mail message. The best way to test out any unfamiliar e-mail features is to send a test message to your own e-mail address. This saves wasting somebody else's time, and the message can be very quickly checked to see the results.

Action the **File**, **New Mail Message** command from any of the main Netscape windows to open the **Message Composition** window, shown below.

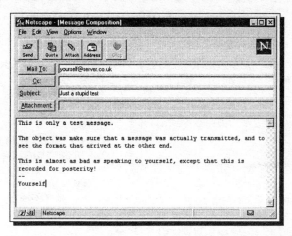

Type your own e-mail address in the **Mail To** field, and a title for the message in the **Subject** field. The text in this subject field will form a header for the message when it is received, so it helps to show in a few words what the message is about. Type your message and when you are happy with it, click the **Send** toolbar icon.

If your Internet connection is open your message will be sent, and should be placed straight into your mailbox. When Netscape next checks for mail, it will find the message and will change the mail icon to that shown here.

Clicking the mail icon, or the **Get Mail** toolbar button, should download your message and place it in the Inbox folder for you to read and marvel!

The Mail Window

The Mail window consists of three panes which, by default, are displayed as shown in our example on page 52. With version 3.0 of the Navigator you can choose one of three pane layouts from the **Appearance** dialogue box opened from the **Options**, **Mail and News Preferences** menu. We will let you try these for yourself.

The Mail Folder Pane:

The mail folder pane contains an alphabetical list of your Mail Folders, very similar to a Bookmark list

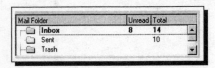

described in an earlier chapter. The Unread column shows the number of unread messages in each folder and Total shows the number of messages within the folder. Text and numbers are displayed bold in this pane if unread messages are contained in their folder.

You can add your own folders with the **File**, **New Folder** menu command from the Mail window and, as long as they are empty, you can delete them with the <Del> key, or the **Edit**, **Delete Folder** command.

The Message Header Pane:

When you select a mail folder, by clicking it in the Mail Folder pane, the Message Header pane shows the contents of that folder. Brief details of each message in the folder are displayed on one line, as shown on the facing page.

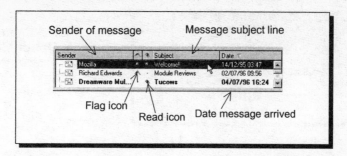

Sender of message   Message subject line

Flag icon

Read icon   Date message arrived

The Sender column normally shows the name of the sender of the mail message, but with version 3.0, in the Outbox and Sent folders, it now more logically, shows the Recipient instead of the Sender, and the column shows the e-mail address of the message recipient.

The **Flag** icon lets you mark, or flag, a message for some future action. Clicking the icon toggles the flag status of the message. The **Read** icon shows that the message has not been viewed. You can click this to toggle the read status. These are important as you can carry out several menu operations on groups of messages in a folder, depending on their Flag and Read status.

If you want to keep a message, when you have read it, you can drag it into one of the folders in the Mail Folder pane.

The Message Content Pane:

When you select a message in the Message Header pane, it is displayed in the Message Content pane which takes up the rest of the window, as shown in our example on page 52.

This shows part of the message that Netscape places when you install the program. It is well worth reading this message, as it highlights some of Mail's excellent features.

A **header** is always placed at the start of a message to help you identify it. You can control how much detail

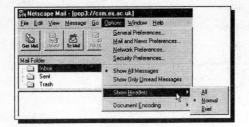

is displayed in this header with the **Options, Show Headers** menu command, as shown here. The default is **Normal**.

Changing the Layout of Panes

You can make any of the three panes bigger or smaller by placing the pointer on one of the central frame borders, holding the left mouse button down and dragging the frame. Drag a vertical frame to the left or right, as shown above, or drag a horizontal frame up or down.

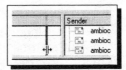

At the same time, you will probably need to adjust the width of columns in the top two panes. This is done in a similar way, but with the mouse pointer located in the title bar of the pane, as shown alongside.

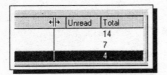

It is best to adjust the size of columns from left to right in a pane, or else you will end up losing some of the column titles, which looks very untidy!

Once you have found the window layout that suits you best, it will be maintained by Netscape, unless you make any changes in the future.

To temporarily sort a list of messages in the Message Header Pane, you can click the mouse pointer in the title of the column you want the list sorted on. The message list is sorted immediately.

The Mail Toolbar

Get Mail — Connects to the mailbox server and downloads waiting messages, which it places in the Inbox folder.

Delete — Deletes the currently selected message and places it in the Trash folder.

To:Mail — Opens the Message Composition window for creating a new mail message, with the To field blank.

Re:Mail — Opens the Message Composition window for replying to the current mail message, with the To field pre-addressed to the original sender.

Re:All — Opens the Message Composition window for replying to the current mail message, with the To field pre-addressed to the original sender as well as all the other recipients of the current message.

Forward — Opens the Message Composition window for forwarding the current mail message as an attachment. The To field is blank. The original Subject field is prefixed with Fwd.

Previous — View the previous unread message in the message list.

Next — View the next unread message in the message list.

Print — Prints the currently selected message.

Stop — Halts any ongoing transmission of messages from the mail server.

Right-Click Menus

As with the rest of the Navigator, if you right-click your mouse in one of the Mail panes a context sensitive menu is opened to give you rapid access to the commands available at the time. Our composite below shows all three of these right-click menus open at the same time, to demonstrate the differences between them.

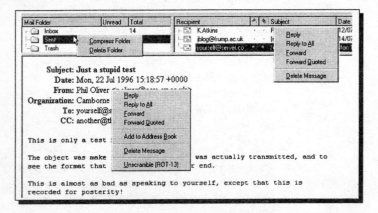

If you look very closely at the above, you will see it was the test message we sent to, in our case the fictitious address 'yourself@server.co.uk'. Yet it still appears in the Sent folder, as if it had actually been transmitted.

One problem with e-mail is that you don't really know, sometimes for several days, if the message actually made it to the recipient, or not. The same is, of course, true with normal mail, so in some ways we are not too much further ahead.

The above illustration also shows the **Normal** headers that are included in a message. Try altering the choices given by the **Options**, **Show Headers** menu command in a message of your own, and see the results.

The View Menu

The Mail **View** menu options are shown here. They allow you to control how your messages are sorted in the list, or whether they are threaded. If you thread your messages, the replies to any you have sent will be linked to the original message, not placed in the list, depending on a sort order.

Some people insist on sending e-mail messages with very long line lengths. With Netscape this is no problem as you can opt for **Wrap Long Lines**. With some other e-mail software line lengths of over 70 characters are truncated. Frustrating, to say the least.

The **Unscramble (ROT13)** option lets you decode messages which have been character coded by the sender. The **Reload** option gets the message from the server again, while **Refresh** simply redraws the message on the screen. **Load Images** displays the images of the current message if they have not been automatically loaded.

Document Source opens a Source window showing the current message page in HTML format, in other words the same as a Web document.

Viewing File Attachments

Until fairly recently, e-mail on the Internet was good only for short text notes. You couldn't send attachments like formatted documents or graphics with your messages. That has now changed with the advent of MIME, which stands for Multipurpose Internet Mail Extension. With the Netscape Navigator you can send

Web pages, other formatted documents, photos, sound and video files as attachments to your main e-mail message. One thing to be careful of though, is make sure that the person you are sending attachments to has e-mail software capable of decoding them.

Inline Attachments:

The **Attachments Inline** menu option lets you view a message attachment at the end of the received message page.

Linked Attachments:

With the **Attachments as Links** option, on the other hand, you have to open a page attachment by clicking a link. If the sender has attached a Web page, a link to it is added to the message body. Clicking on the link displays the Web page in the Message Content pane.

Folder Maintenance

Most of the other menu options in the main Mail window are concerned with keeping and updating your folders of e-mail messages.

Emptying the Trash:

Whenever you delete a message it is actually moved to the Trash folder. This, of course, gets bigger and bigger over time. When you are sure you will not want any of its contained messages again, you use the **File**, **Empty Trash Folder** command to finally delete them.

Compressing Empty Space:

As you delete messages you create empty space on your hard disc drive and the status bar shows details of the wasted space in the currently open folder. To remove it you should action the **File**, **Compress Folder** menu command every now and then.

Selecting Messages:

When you have a lot of messages to handle, several of the options in the **Edit** menu can be useful.

- **Select Thread** selects all messages in the current thread, these are ones connected by the same theme.
- **Select Flagged Messages** highlights messages in the current thread that have been marked in the Flag column of the Message Header pane.
- As you would expect, **Select All Messages** selects all messages in all of your threads.

Working with Flagged Files:

By flagging any group of messages you want to work with in the Message Header pane, you can then use the above commands to select, or highlight, them and then process them in some specific way. This may entail deleting them, or copying or moving them to a specific folder for instance.

The Message Composition Window

We briefly looked into the Message Composition window earlier in the chapter. This is the window, shown on the next page, that you will use to create any messages you want to send electronically from Netscape, whether from the Mail or the News sections. It is very important to understand its features, so that you can get the most out of it.

As we saw, it can be opened by using the **File**, **New Mail Message** command from any of the main Netscape windows, but perhaps the easiest way from the Mail window is by clicking the **To:Mail** toolbar icon shown here.

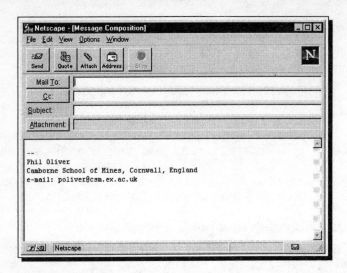

As shown above, if you have created a signature file and pointed to it in the **Options**, **Mail and News Preferences**, **Identity** dialogue box, the text in the signature file is placed at the end of the message creation area. You could create a signature file in a text editor like Notepad, or WordPad, including only the text and characters you want added to all your messages.

Message Recipients:

With the Netscape Navigator you have a very extensive choice of who will receive copies of any e-mail messages you send. This is controlled in the **View** menu as shown here.

Any of the nine options ticked in the centre panel of this menu will cause a text field to be open in the Message Composition window. By default, only the four shown here are ticked.

The window shown on the facing page, however, has all of the recipient options open. We don't think there will be many times when this will be necessary.

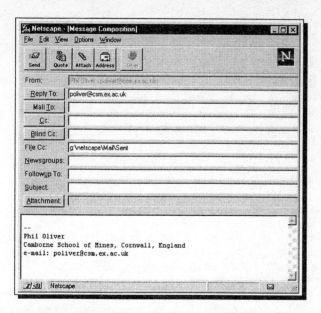

Some of the menu options are not very obvious, so we
have described them all here. Most of the fields can
contain more than one address.

Fro**m**	Shows your e-mail address.
Reply To	Enter the e-mail address where you want any replies sent.
Mail T**o**	Enter the e-mail address(es) of the main recipient(s).
Mail C**c**	Enter the address where you want a copy of your message sent.
Mail B**cc**	Enter the address where you want a blind copy of your message sent. There will be no evidence of this copy on the original message.
Fil**e Cc**	Shows the location on your hard disc where a copy of the message will be stored.

Newsgroups	Enter the name of the newsgroup where you want to post a news message. This is often pre-set.
Followup To	Enter the name of the newsgroup where you want replies to your message posted.
Subject	Enter a short description of your message. This field may be pre-set for you.
Attac**h**ment	Shows the page, or file, name of any attachments.

Adding Attachments

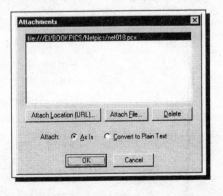

If you want to send a Web page, or other type of file as an attachment to your main e-mail message you simply click the **Attach** toolbar button to open the Attachments box, shown here.

In this you click the **Attach File** button, and select the file(s) to attach, as shown. To add a Web page click the **Attach Location (URL)** button and specify the location address of the page to attach in the opened box. If you want the Web page to maintain its HTML code, make sure the **As Is** option is checked. If you want the page sent as text, without the formatting and links, check the **Convert to Plain Text** option. When you have added all the attachments you want, click on **OK** to return to the Composition window.

Sending an E-mail

When you have filled in the address fields and typed the body of your message you simply click the **Send** toolbar button, shown here, to start the transmission process straight away.

Deferring Delivery:

If you want to keep the message and send it later, maybe with several others to save on your telephone bill, you can first select **Deferred Delivery** from the **Options** menu. When this is selected the **Send** toolbar icon has a small clock face attached to it, as we show here. Clicking this icon places the message in the **Outbox** folder (in the Mail Folder pane), which it creates, if necessary.

When you are ready to send your deferred messages you use the **File**, **Send Messages in Outbox** command, or the <Ctrl+H> keyboard shortcut. If you forget to do this, Netscape will prompt you with this message box when you attempt to exit the program.

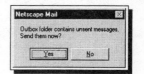

Netscape Mail

Outbox folder contains unsent messages. Send them now?

Yes   No

Replying to a Message

When you receive an e-mail message that you want to reply to, Netscape makes it very easy to do. The reply address and the new message subject fields are both added automatically for you. Also, by default, the original message is quoted in the reply window for you to edit as required.

With the message you want to reply to open in the Mail window, either click the **Re:Mail** toolbar button, use the **Message**, **Reply** menu command, or use the <Ctrl+R> keyboard shortcut. All open the Message Composition window.

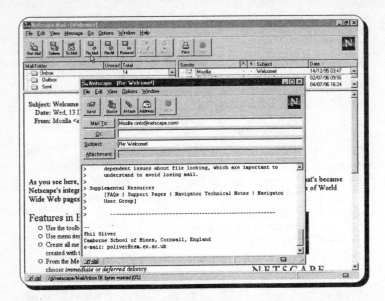

In our example above, we have set up the Navigator to reply to Netscape's opening message. Note the two address fields have automatically been completed, the original message is quoted and our signature file has been added to the end of the message composition area.

Using Quoted Text:

It is almost an e-mail standard now to place the '>' character at the beginning of every line of quoted text in a message. Netscape does this automatically for you, as you can see above. You should not, however, leave all of the original message in your reply. This is very bad practice, which rapidly makes new messages very large and time consuming to download. You should edit the quoted text, so that it is obvious what you are referring to. Usually one or two lines is enough.

If you need the original quoted text to be pasted again while you are preparing the reply, you can click the **Quote** button on the Message Composition toolbar.

The Address Book

E-mail addresses are often quite complicated and not easy to remember at all. With the Navigator there is a very useful Address Book built in and our almost empty one is shown here.

This can be opened from any Netscape window with the **Window**, **Address Book** menu command, and is similar to the Book-marks feature covered in an early chapter.

You can manually add an e-mail address, as long as you know it, of course, with the **Item**, **Add User** menu command. This opens the Properties box, where you enter the users **Nick Name**, **Name**, and **E-Mail Address**, almost the same as with Bookmarks.

The easiest way to add a new entry to the list is to right-click your mouse in the body of a received e-mail message and select the **Add to Address Book** menu item. This opens the Properties box with the details of the sender of the current message already entered. You complete the entry to add the item.

To send a new message to anyone listed in your Address Book you just double-click on their entry, which opens the Composition window, with their details already added.

The **Address** icon in the Composition window, opens the box on the right. You can select a user and click one of the field buttons below, to place the user's address in the **To**, **Copy**, or **Blind Copy** field of your message.

5. MICROSOFT EXPLORER MAIL

Microsoft have included a very good e-mail program with the current version 3 of their Web browser. We enjoyed using this part of the Explorer, but had some reservations about the browser itself. That is obviously the problem with such a very large 'disc hungry' package. To justify its space on your PC you have to use most of its features.

Getting Your Browser

When you are actually connected to the Internet you can download Microsoft's Internet Explorer software absolutely free of charge.

If you are not yet connected, you may have to shop around for the software. Some computer magazines, especially those on the Internet, come with a CD-ROM attached. Frequently Microsoft use this method of distributing their latest free software. If you can find one with the latest version of the Internet Explorer, buy it and follow the instructions to install the package.

Downloading the Internet Explorer:

We will outline the procedure for downloading the Internet Explorer version 3.1 for Windows 95.

You can access the Microsoft Download page by clicking a Download Area button from a Web page, or by entering the following URL address into your browser.

http://www.microsoft.com/ie/download/

This is the US based page you can start from whenever you want to download any Microsoft browser software.

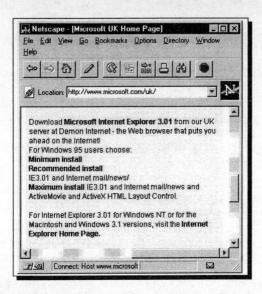

A much faster option, but one we find is sometimes not active, is to open Microsoft's UK site at:

http://www.microsoft.com/uk/

Click the **Recommended install** link, as shown above. This includes Mail and Newsreader features along with the Web browser.

Clicking the filename entry link, and giving a file saving location when asked, will start the transfer process. It is always a good idea to have a temporary storage area on your hard disc for these occasions. Ours is a folder, or directory, called *temp*.

The browser file you selected, named something like MSIE301R.EXE, should eventually arrive in your temporary folder, but this procedure can be very slow, especially if the download is from the US.

Installing the Internet Explorer:

Double-clicking the down-loaded .EXE program file from a Windows 95 'My Computer' window will start the installation procedure.

If you are asked whether you want to control which parts of the Explorer suite are installed, make sure you select to install the Mail part of the program. When the installation procedure is finished you will be asked to restart your computer by clicking the **Yes** button. If you did not have enough space on your hard disc, you will be told to free up more room and try again. Good luck.

Starting the Explorer

The Internet

When your system starts up again you will find a new Internet icon has been placed on your Desktop. Double-clicking this icon for the first time will start the Internet Connection Wizard which will step you through the process of establishing your link to the Internet.

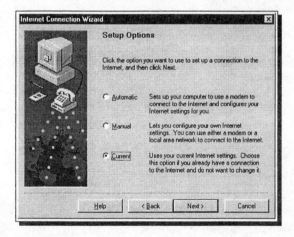

If you have a modem this Wizard can make the process of setting up your connection quite painless. We were not impressed however with the facilities for connecting up via a Local Area Network. Obviously how you complete the options that are offered will depend on your particular system and circumstances.

Using Microsoft Mail

To start the Mail program, click the **Mail** Explorer Toolbar icon and then select **Read Mail** from the menu that opens, as shown on the left.

Before you can use your browser to send, or receive, mail you have to tell the program how to connect to your server's facilities. You can do this in two ways. By completing your personal e-mail connection details in the Internet Mail Configuration Wizard, which opens when you first attempt to use the Mail program.

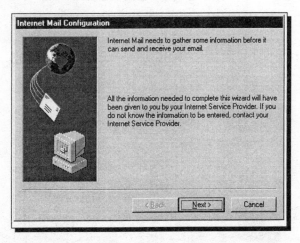

The other way, if the Mail window opens but your details are not correct, is to use the options box, shown on the next page, which is opened when the **Mail**, **Options**, menu command is actioned from the Mail window, and the **Server** tab is clicked.

To complete the details in this box you may need to ask your Internet service provider or system administrator for your details. The ones shown here will obviously only work for the writer.

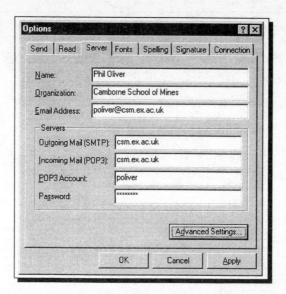

You type your e-mail name (only the part that precedes the @ sign in your e-mail address) into the **POP3 Account** text field. Without this, Explorer will not know which mailbox to look in! The password to enter, in the **Password** field, is the one to open the mailbox on your server. Details of this should have been given to you by your Internet service provider or system administrator when you opened your 'service account'. When you have finished, press **OK** to close the box and save your changes.

The first time the Mail window opens, a message from Microsoft, which has been saved on your hard disc, is displayed, as shown at the top of the next page.

To check your own mail, click the **Send and Receive** Toolbar icon which will download any new messages from your mailbox to your hard disc. You can then read and process your mail at your leisure without necessarily being still connected to the Internet.

With the default set-up, Explorer will only check your mailbox when you click the **Send and Receive** icon.

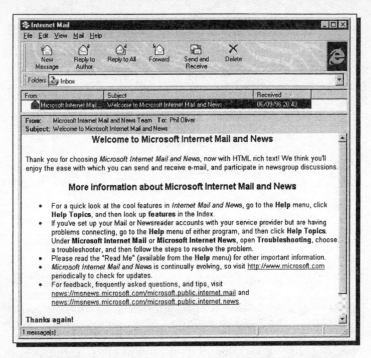

We suggest you make a change in the **Mail**, **Options**,
Read tab settings sheet. Selecting the **Check for new
messages every 10
minutes** option will make
the program check your
mail box when it starts
and at regular intervals
while it is open.

A Trial Run

Before explaining in more detail the features of
Explorer Mail we will step through the procedure of
sending a very simple e-mail message. The best way
to test out any unfamiliar e-mail features is to send a
test message to your own e-mail address. This saves
wasting somebody else's time, and the message can
be very quickly checked to see the results.

Click the **New Message** Toolbar icon to open the window, shown below.

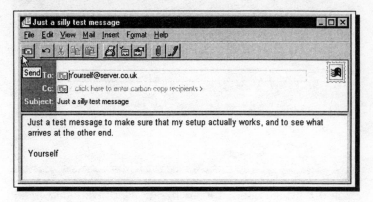

Type your own e-mail address in the **To:** field, and a title for the message in the **Subject:** field. The text in this subject field will form a header for the message when it is received, so it helps to show in a few words what the message is about. Type your message and when you are happy with it, click the **Send** toolbar icon.

The box shown here may then display to explain what has happened to your message. By default, it is stored in an Outbox folder, and pressing the **Send and Receive** Toolbar icon will send it, hopefully straight into your mailbox. When Explorer next checks for mail, it will find the message and download it into the Inbox folder, as shown on the next page, for you to read and enjoy!

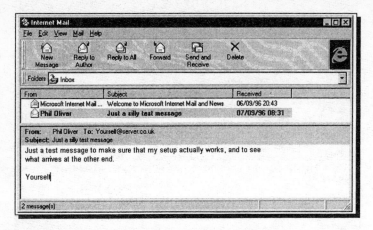

Explorer Mail uses three main windows, the Mail
window, which opens first; the Read Message window
for reading your mail; and the Send Message window,
to compose your outgoing mail messages.

The Mail Window

The Mail window consists of a Toolbar and three panes
with the default display shown in our example above.
You can choose different pane layouts with the **View**,
Preview Pane menu command, and you can drag the
Toolbar display as in the main Explorer window. We
will let you try these for yourself.

The Folders Pane:

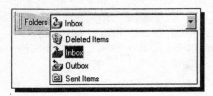

The mail folders
pane contains an
alphabetical list of
your Mail Folders.
There are always at
least four of these,
as shown, but you
can add your own
folders with the **File**, **Folder**, **Create** menu command
from the Mail window. As long as your added folders

are empty, you can delete them again with the **File**, **Folder**, **Delete** command.

The Header Pane:

When you select a folder, by clicking it in the Folders pane, the Header pane shows the contents of that folder. Brief details of each message are displayed on one line, as shown on the previous page.

The 'From' column shows the name of the sender of the mail message; 'Subject' shows the title of each mail message, and 'Received' shows the date it reached you. You can control what columns display in this pane with the **View**, **Columns** menu command. The other options are, 'Sent' which shows the sending date and time of the message, 'Size' which gives its file size, and 'To', which shows who it was addressed to.

To sort a list of messages in the Header Pane, you can click the mouse pointer in the title of the column you want the list sorted on.

If you want to keep a message when you have read it, you can use either the **Move to**, or **Copy to** commands from the **Mail** menu to store it in one of the folders in the Folder pane.

The Preview Pane:

When you select a message in the Header pane, by clicking it once, it is displayed in the Preview pane, which takes up the rest of the window. This lets you read the first few lines to see if the message is worth bothering with. If so, double clicking the header, in the Header pane, will open the message in the Read Message window, as shown later in the chapter.

You could use the Preview pane to read all your mail, especially if your messages are all on the short side, but it is easier to process them from the Read Message window.

The Mail Window Toolbar:

 Opens the Send Message window for creating a new mail message, with the To: field blank.

 Opens the Send Message window for replying to the current mail message, with the To: field pre-addressed to the original sender.

 Opens the Send Message window for replying to the current mail message, with the To: field pre-addressed to all that received copies of the original message.

 Opens the Send Message window for forwarding the current mail message. The To: field is blank. The original Subject field is prefixed with Fw:.

 Connects to the mailbox server and downloads waiting messages, which it places in the Inbox folder. Sends any messages waiting in the Outbox folder.

 Deletes the currently selected message and places it in the Deleted Items folder.

The Read Message Window

If you double-click a message in the Header pane of the Mail window the Read Message window is opened, as shown below.

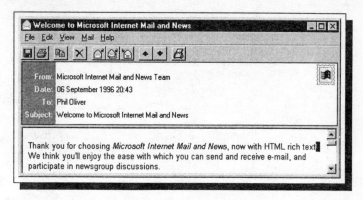

This is the best window to read your mail in. It has its own menu system and Toolbar, which lets you rapidly process and move between the messages in a folder.

The Read Message Toolbar:

 Opens the Save Message As box for you to save the message to a disc file. The possible disc formats are, .txt for an ASCII text file, or .eml for a Mail file.

 Sends the message to the current Windows printer and uses all the default print settings.

 Copies selected text to the Windows clipboard.

Deletes the current message, places it in the Deleted Items folder, and closes the Read Message window.

 Opens the Send Message window for replying to the current mail message, with the To: field pre-addressed to the original sender.

 Opens the Send Message window for replying to the current mail message, with the To: field pre-addressed to all that received message copies.

 Opens the Send Message window for forwarding the current mail message. The To: field is blank. The original Subject field is prefixed with Fw:.

 Displays the previous mail message in the Read Message window. The button appears depressed if there are no previous messages.

 Displays the next mail message in the Read Message window. The button appears depressed if there are no more messages.

 Opens the Address Book window for you to add the details of the message sender.

Viewing File Attachments

Until fairly recently, e-mail on the Internet was good only for short text notes. You couldn't send attachments like formatted document or graphic files with your messages. That has now changed with the advent of MIME, which stands for Multipurpose Internet Mail Extension. With the Internet Explorer you can send Web pages, other formatted documents, photos, sound and video files as attachments to your main e-mail message.

One thing to be careful of though, is to make sure that the person you are sending attachments to has e-mail software capable of decoding them.

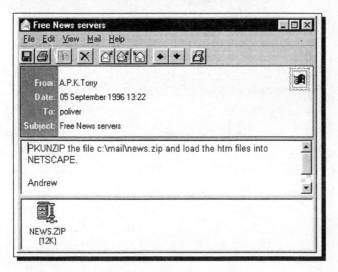

The file attachment appears at the bottom of the message in the Read Message window. To view, or run the file, double-click its icon.

To save a file attachment, use the **File**, **Save Attachments** menu command.

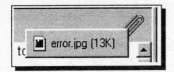

To display, or run, an attachment from the preview pane, click the paper clip file attachment icon in the preview pane header, and then click the file name. To save it from the preview pane, hold down the <Ctrl> key when you click the displayed file name.

The Send Message Window

We briefly looked into the Send Message window earlier in the chapter. This is the window, shown below, that you will use to create any messages you want to send electronically from Explorer, whether from the Mail or the News sections. It is very important to understand its features, so that you can get the most out of it.

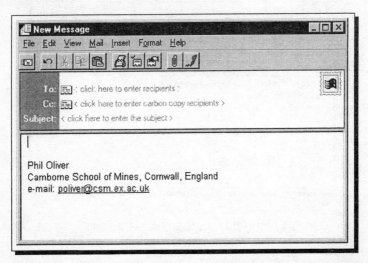

As we saw, this window can be opened by using the **New Message** Toolbar icon, as well as the **Mail, New Message** menu command, or the <Ctrl+N> keyboard shortcut from the main Mail window.

It has its own menu system and Toolbar, which let you rapidly prepare and send your new e-mail messages.

Your Own Signature :

If you have created a signature in the **Mail**, **Options**, **Signature** box, as shown below, its text is placed at the end of the message creation area.

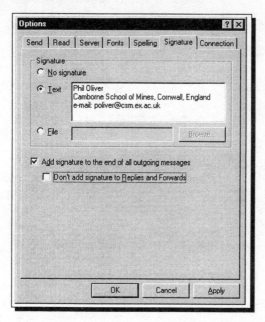

You could also create a more fancy signature file in a text editor like Notepad, or WordPad, including the text and characters you want added to all your messages, and point to it in the **File** section of this box.

We have chosen to **Add signature to the end of all outgoing messages**, but you could leave this option blank and use the **Signature** Toolbar icon if you prefer.

The Send Message Toolbar:

 Sends the created message, either to the recipient, or to the Outbox folder, depending on your settings in the **Mail**, **Options**, **Send** box.

 Undoes the last editing action.

 Cuts selected text to the Windows clipboard.

 Copies selected text to the Windows clipboard.

 Pastes the contents of the Windows clipboard into the current message, at the insertion point.

 Opens the Address Book.

 Checks that any names match your entries in the address book, or are in the correct e-mail address format (name@company).

 Opens the Select Recipients window (which is linked to the Address Book) for you to select who should receive the message.

 Opens the Insert Attachment window for you to select a file to be attached to the current message.

Adds your signature to the bottom of the message, as long as you have specified one in the **Mail**, **Options**, **Signature** box.

Message Formatting

Mail provides quite sophisticated formatting options for an e-mail editor from the **Format** menu, as shown below. These only work if you prepare the message in HTML format, as used in Web documents.

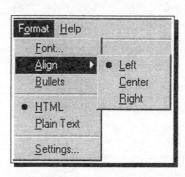

In the **Mail**, **Options**, **Send** box you can set this to be your default mail sending format. To use the format for the current message only, select **HTML** from the **Format** menu, as we have done here.

With HTML, the above Format Toolbar is added to the Send Message window and the top three menu options are then made active. The **Font** command gives you full control of the message font type, and its size and attributes. These functions are also provided by the first six Format Toolbar buttons

The **Align** command, and the three right Toolbar buttons, let you format your message paragraphs with **Left**, **Center** or **Right** alignment.

 The **Bullets** menu option, or the Toolbar button shown here, give you an indented bulleted paragraph style suitable for using with lists.

All of these formatting features are quite well demonstrated in Microsoft's opening message to you, which we showed on page 79. You should be able to prepare some very easily readable e-mail messages with these features.

Setting Message Priority

Outgoing e-mail messages can be given one of three priority ratings, so that their recipients can rank their mail in order of importance. This is only of any real use, though, if the person receiving the message can use the facility.

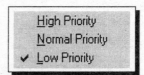

To set message priorities, either use the **Mail**, **Set Priority** command, or right-click the postage stamp-like icon in the Send Message window. Both open the three choice menu, shown above, the options of which change the stamp icon on the message to one of the following.

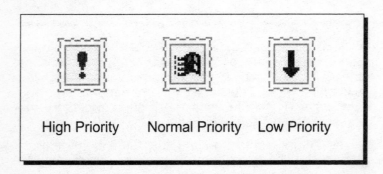

High Priority   Normal Priority   Low Priority

Adding Attachments

If you want to send a Web page, or other type of file as an attachment to your main e-mail message you simply click the **Insert Attachment** Toolbar button and select the file to attach.

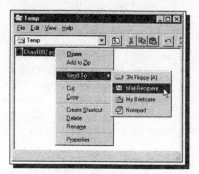

There is an easy way of doing this with Windows 95. You may have noticed that when Internet Mail was installed on your system the new option **Mail Recipient** was placed on your **Send To** menu.

To try this out, open a My Computer window and right-click on a file (any file, it doesn't matter which one). You may have more, or less, options than shown in our example above (depending on your system set-up), but you should have Mail Recipient. Clicking this opens a Send Message window with the attachment file added to the bottom, as shown below.

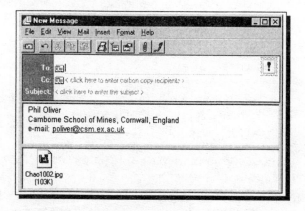

Sending an E-mail

 When you have filled in the address fields, typed and formatted the body of your message, added any attachments, and maybe placed a signature, you simply click the **Send** Toolbar button, shown here, to start the transmission process. What happens to the message next depends on your Option settings.

If you want to keep the message and send it later, maybe with several others to save on your telephone bill, make sure the **Send messages immediately** option is not selected in the **Mail**, **Options**, **Send** settings box. In this case, clicking the above **Send** Toolbar icon places the message in the Outbox folder.

When you are ready to send your held messages you click the **Send and Receive** Toolbar icon on the main Mail window. If you forget to do this, Explorer will prompt you with a message box when you attempt to exit the program.

When the **Send messages immediately** option is selected, your messages will be sent on their way as soon as you click the **Send** Toolbar button. This option is best used if you have a permanent connection to the Internet, or your e-mail is being sent over an internal network, or Intranet.

Replying to a Message

When you receive an e-mail message that you want to reply to, Explorer Mail makes it very easy to do. The reply address and the new message subject fields are both added automatically for you. Also, by default, the original message is quoted in the reply window for you to edit as required.

With the message you want to reply to open in the Mail window, either click the **Reply to Author** Toolbar button, use the **Mail**, **Reply to Author** menu command, or use the <Ctrl+R> keyboard shortcut. All open the Send Message window.

Using Quoted Text:

It is almost an e-mail standard now to place the '>' character at the beginning of every line of quoted text in a message. Explorer does this automatically for you.

You should not, however, leave all of the original message in your reply. This is very bad practice, which rapidly makes new messages very large and time consuming to download. You should edit the quoted text, so that it is obvious what you are referring to. Usually one or two lines is enough.

Removing Deleted Messages

Whenever you delete a message it is actually moved to the Deleted Items folder. If ignored, this folder gets

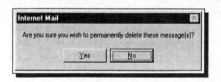 bigger and bigger over time, so you need to either check it every few days and manually re-delete messages you are sure you will

not need again. In which case you are given this last warning message. Or, if you are confident that you will not need this safety net, you can opt to **Empty messages from the 'Deleted Items' folder on exit** in the **Mail**, **Options**, **Read** settings box. You will then have a short time to change your mind before they are finally deleted.

The Address Book

E-mail addresses are often quite complicated and not easy to remember at all. With the Explorer there is a very useful Address Book built in and an almost empty example of one is shown here.

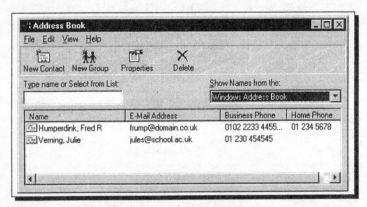

It can be opened from the main Explorer window with the **File**, **Address Book** menu command, or from the Read and Send Message windows by clicking the **Address Book** Toolbar icon.

You can manually add a person's full details and e-mail address, in the Properties box that opens when you click the **New Contact** Toolbar icon. The **New Group** icon lets you create a grouping of e-mail addresses, you can then send mail to everyone in the group with one operation.

We will leave it to you to find your way round this very comprehensive facility. Don't forget that it has its own Help system that you can use.

To send a new message to anyone listed in your Address Book, open a Send Message window and click the **Select Recipients** Toolbar icon, which is shown here.

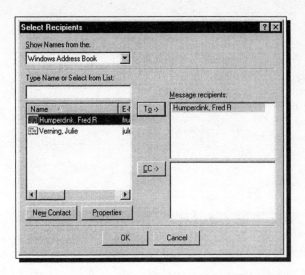

In this window you can select a person's name and click either the **To**-> button to place it in the **To:** field of your message, or the **CC->** button to place it in the **Cc:** field.

The **New Contact** button lets you add details for a new person to the Address Book, and the **Properties** button lets you edit an existing entry.

The Inbox Assistant

If you are ever in the situation of receiving e-mail messages from a source you do not want to hear from, you can use the Inbox Assistant to filter your incoming messages. Unwanted ones can be placed in your Deleted Items folder straight away. It is also useful for sorting incoming messages and automatically routing them to their correct folders.

To open the Assistant, which is shown on the next page, use the **Mail**, **Inbox Assistant** menu command. Click the **Add** button and type the criteria you want the incoming message to match in the Properties box.

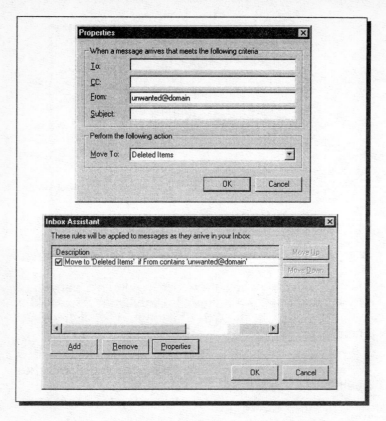

In our example above, we have set the Assistant to intercept any messages from 'unwanted@domain' and send them for immediate deletion.

You can set multiple rules for incoming messages and control the priority that messages are sorted in the list. The higher up a multiple list a condition is the higher will be its priority. Use the **Move Up** and **Move Down** buttons to change priorities.

If an incoming message matches more than one rule, then it is sorted according to the first rule it matches in your list.

6. EUDORA LIGHT FOR WINDOWS 95

One of the older versions of Eudora was the e-mail program we first started on, but the latest freeware version for Windows 95, or Windows NT, is far

superior. We have no hesitation in recommending this program. It is provided by QUALCOMM Incorporated, who "grant the user a nonexclusive license to use this Eudora Software solely for their own personal or internal business purposes". It is, in fact, a cut-down version of their commercial program Eudora Pro. They have removed the ability to format and spell check your messages, and have de-activated many of the message filtering actions. It is still a package worth having, though.

Some Eudora Features

At the time of writing, Version 3.0.1 was the latest release of Eudora Light for Windows NT and Windows 95. Some of its features include:

- The ability to **drag and drop** messages between folders and mailboxes.

- Displays **Text formatting** features, including different font sizes, colours and layout options.

- Web links - **URLs** - are highlighted in a message, double-clicking them will activate your web browser.

- **Long filename support** for Windows 95 and Windows NT.

- Can automatically keep **copies** of all your outgoing mail.

- **Mail filtering** automates your mail processing.

- Extensive **address book** features with aliasing.

- A comprehensive context-sensitive on-line **Help** system.

- Comprehensive support for the **Internet MIME** multimedia messaging standard.

- **MAPI** support allows the sending of messages from within MAPI-enabled applications, such as word processors or spreadsheets.

- Can be used with the **Kerberos Authentication System** for increased message security.

Getting the software

You can often find Eudora on the CD-ROMs attached to Internet magazines, or you can download from Qualcomm's web site at the following URL address:

```
http://www.eudora.com/light.html
```

This opened the window shown below when we accessed it last. It may not still be the same though!

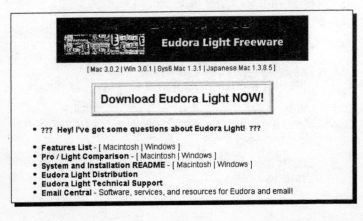

94

We found our version at one of our favourite sources of Internet software, Tucows mentioned in an earlier chapter, which has the UK mirror site shown below. This makes the downloading operation very quick indeed, especially during the middle of the day.

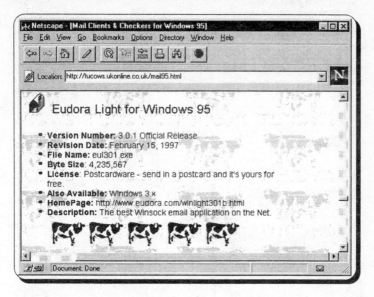

To download the program file, first access the above site with your Web browser by typing the URL address shown in the **Location** text box. Then, simply clicking the Eudora Light for Windows 95 link, and giving a file saving location when asked, will start the transfer process. It is always a good idea to have a temporary storage area on your hard disc for these occasions. Ours is a directory, or folder, called *temp*.

Installing Eudora Light

Double-clicking the downloaded program file - EUL301.EXE - in a Windows 95 Explorer window, will start installing the program. This self-extracts the files

and loads a Set-up Wizard which steps you easily
through the whole installation.

Starting Eudora

When you next open your Windows 95 START menu
you will find a new item in the
Programs section, as shown
here. To start the program,
click this **Eudora Light** option.

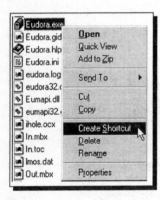

You could, of course, create
a Shortcut icon, by opening
the Eudora folder in a My
Computer window, right
clicking on the
EUDORA.EXE file, and
selecting the **Create
Shortcut** option,
as shown here.
Then just drag
the shortcut icon
onto your
desktop.

Shortcut to
Eudora.exe

The first time Eudora opened on our PC it displayed
the box shown below. If you have upgraded from a
previous version you will probably not see it. Select
Yes to have a first look at the Eudora window.

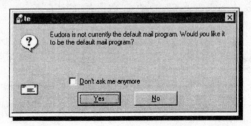

96

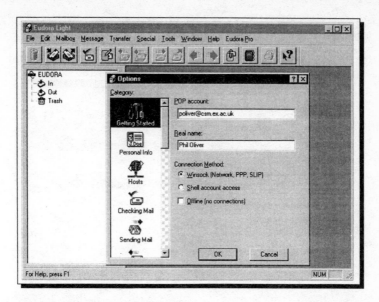

Before you can use Eudora to send, or receive, mail you have to tell the program how to connect to your server's facilities. You do this in the box above that automatically opens if its details have not been filled in.

Eudora have made this operation very easy, but you can always ask your Internet service provider or system administrator for your details. The ones shown here will obviously only work for the writer.

In the **POP account** field you enter your login name for your POP3 server account, an "@" sign, and the full (domain) name of the computer; in most cases this will actually be your e-mail address.

Type your actual name in the **Real Name** field. What you type here, will be displayed in brackets after your return address, and in the sender column, of all your outgoing mail messages.

To get help on any item in an Options box, click the '?' button and then click the Help cursor on the item. When you have finished, press **OK** to close the box and save your changes.

The first time Eudora is opened it contains a message, from Qualcomm which was saved on your hard disc during the installation.

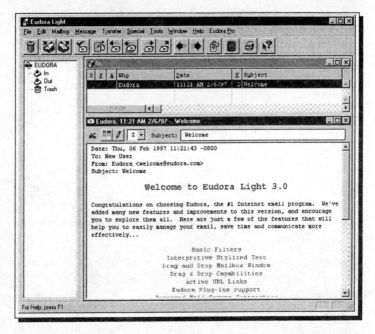

 To find this message, double-click the **In** entry in the Mailbox window on the left of the Eudora window, or click the **Open In mailbox** icon, shown here; both of these open the 'In' mailbox window. Select the message in this window and double-click it.

To check your own mail, click the **Get mail** icon, shown below, or use the **File**, **Check Mail** menu command, or use the <Ctrl+M> quick key combination.

 All of these will download any new messages from your mailbox to your hard disc. You can then read and process your mail at your leisure without necessarily being still connected to the Internet.

98

With the default set-up, Eudora will only check your mailbox when you ask it to. You can force it to check your mail at regular intervals in the **Tools**, **Options**, **Checking Mail** settings sheet. Setting the **Check for mail every** 10 **minutes** option, as shown below, will make the program check your mail box when it starts and at ten minute intervals while it is open.

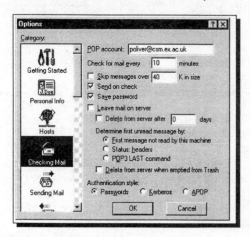

Before making any changes in one of these configuration sheets we strongly recommend that you click the '?' Help button and study the options available.

A Trial Run

Before explaining in more detail the main features of Eudora Light we will step through the procedure of sending a very simple e-mail message. The best way to test out any unfamiliar e-mail features is to send a test message to your own e-mail address. This saves wasting somebody else's time, and the message can be very quickly checked to see the results.

Click the **New message** icon, to open the message editor window, shown on the next page.

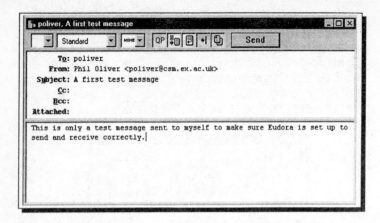

Type your own e-mail address in the **To:** field, and a title for the message in the **Subject:** field. The text in this subject field will form a header for the message when it is received, so it helps to show in a few words what the message is about. Note how the Title bar of the window changes to this information. Type your message and when you are happy with it, click the **Send/Queue** icon.

By default, outgoing messages are stored in a queue, and are only sent at a time depending on your settings. You can change these settings for a message, in the dialogue box shown here, which is opened if the <Shift> key is depressed when the **Send** button is clicked.

When messages are actually sent, is controlled in the **Tools**, **Options**, **Sending Mail** settings sheet. You can choose between **Immediate send**, or **Send on check**.

When Eudora next checks for mail, it will hopefully find the message and download it into the 'In' mailbox, for you to open and read, as shown below.

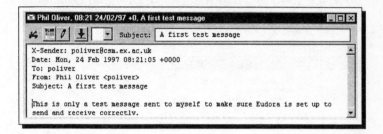

The Help System

At last Eudora now has a comprehensive built-in Help system. Before you go too much further we suggest you check this out with the **Help**, **Topics** menu command. This opens a standard Windows 95 Help window. Working through the Contents section, as shown below, will quickly introduce you to the main features of Eudora.

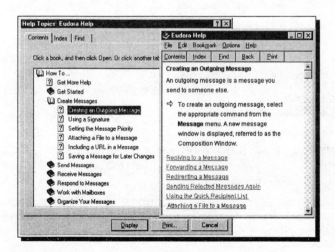

Quitting Eudora

When you have finished working with Eudora, you can close the program with the **File**, **Exit** menu command, the <Ctrl+Q> key strokes, or by clicking its 'X' close window button.

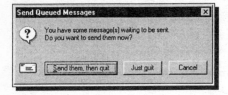

If you have any unsent messages in the queue, you will be asked what you want doing with them, as shown here.

Passwords

The next time you open Eudora and check your mail, you will need to enter your password in the Password dialogue box shown here. This is the Password required to open your mailbox on your server. Simply type in your password and click **OK**.

If your computer is in a secure place and you are not worried about anybody else reading your mail, you can force Eudora to remember your password from one session to the next. To do this turn on **Save password** in the **Tools**, **Options**, **Checking Mail** settings sheet. You would then not have to enter your password again, even if you exit and restart Eudora.

You may also be able to change your POP account password from Eudora, with the **Special**, **Change Password** command. It did not work with us though!

The Eudora Window

The Main window, as shown below, contains the program's menu, tool and status bars as well as the Mailboxes window.

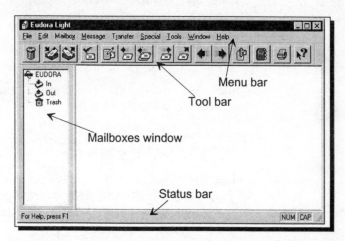

As you would expect, you can control all of Eudora's features by selecting options from the menu system, or by clicking an icon on the tool bar.

As you move the selection through the menu bar options, a one-line description of the currently selected option shows on the status bar.

The Mailboxes window gives you control over your mailboxes and folders. On start up it contains the three system mailboxes shown above, and it is automatically 'docked' to the left side of the Eudora window.

To move the Mailboxes window, hold down the left mouse button on the rim of the window and drag it to where you want it. You can place it anywhere on the Windows desktop. When you drag it slowly over the left or right edge of the Eudora window, the dragged 'outline' changes shape and on releasing the mouse button it will re-dock in a vertical position.

The Main Tool Bar:

 Delete Message and place it in the Trash mailbox.

 Open In Mailbox and display its contents.

 Open Out Mailbox and display its contents.

 Check Mail at the mailbox server and download it to the In mailbox.

 Open the Composition window for creating a **New Message**.

 Open the Composition window for you to **Reply** to the current mail message, with the To field pre-addressed to the original sender.

 Reply To All - Opens the Composition window for replying to the current mail message, with the To field pre-addressed to the original sender and all the other recipients of the current message.

 Forward - Opens the Composition window for forwarding the current message. The To field is blank and the original text is quoted in the body of the new message.

 Redirect - Lets you send the current message unchanged to somebody else.

 Open Previous message in the mailbox.

Open Next message in the mailbox.

 Attach File to the current message.

 Opens the **Address Book**.

 Print the currently selected message, as well as some Eudora windows.

 Gives **Help** for clicked on menu items, icons and windows.

Right-Click Menus:

As with most Windows programs these days, if you right-click your mouse in an object, or a window, a context sensitive menu is opened to give you rapid access to the commands available at the time. Our composite below shows some of these right-click menus open at the same time.

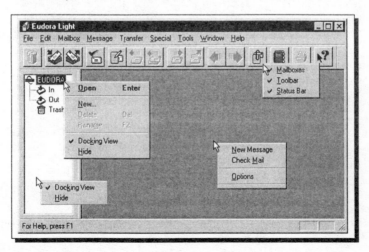

The Mailboxes Window

The Mailboxes window contains a graphical alphabetical listing of all your mailboxes. The three there to start with are named, In, Out and Trash. These are system boxes in which your incoming mail, outgoing mail and deleted mail messages are stored. Double-clicking on one opens the actual mailbox.

You can add your own message storage folders with the **Mailbox**, **New** menu command, or by selecting **New** from the Mailboxes window right-click menu, as shown on the previous page.

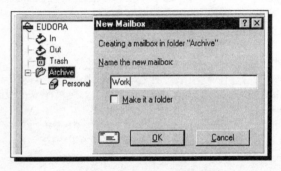

In our example above, we named a new mailbox 'Archive' and selected to **Make it a folder**. Folders can contain their own boxes which lets you build a structured list, as shown here. You rename and delete your own created folders and mailboxes in the normal Windows 95 way, but you cannot change the system ones.

If you 'lose' the Mailboxes window at any time, you have probably hidden it. Don't worry, you can get it back with the **Tools**, **View Mailboxes** command.

Mailbox Windows

When you open a mailbox, by double-clicking it in the Mailboxes window, the contents of the mailbox are shown in a listing. Brief details of each message in the box are displayed on one line, as shown below.

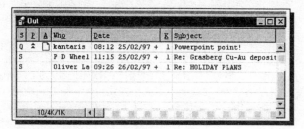

Each message summary is divided into columns, as shown above. From left to right these show a message's, **S**tatus, **P**riority, **A**ttachments, Sender/ Recipient details, Date, Size, and Subject.

Status Indicators:

The indicator in the 'S' column tells you the current status of a message. In an incoming mailbox the indicators are different from those in an outgoing one, as shown below.

Outgoing		Incoming	
	Unsendable	•	Unread
•	Sendable		Read
Q	Queued	R	Replied to
T	Time queued	F	Forwarded
S	Sent	D	Redirected
-	Unsent		

107

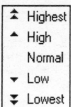

⤒	Highest
▲	High
	Normal
▼	Low
⤓	Lowest

The 'P' column shows the Priority, or importance, that has been put on individual messages by their senders, as shown here.

Both the Status and the Priority of a message can be changed directly in the mailbox window, by right-clicking it and selecting from the opened menu.

The program gives you a lot of control over the display in a mailbox window. You can show, or hide, mailbox columns using the **Tools**, **Options**, **Mailbox Columns** settings sheet, or adjust the width of a column, by dragging its border left or right in the column header. You can sort a list of messages on the contents of any of the columns, by clicking the mouse in that column's header.

The Message Window

When you double-click a message in a mailbox window, it is opened in the Message window, as shown in our example on page 98.

This shows part of the message that Eudora places when you install the program. It is well worth reading this message, as it highlights some of program's excellent features. A header is always placed at the start of a message to help you identify it.

By now you probably have several different Eudora windows open at once. You can control the position and size of all of them in the usual Windows way. You make them bigger or smaller by dragging the pointer on their borders, and move them by dragging them around the screen by their title bar.

Once you have found the window layout that suits you best, maybe like ours on page 98, it will be maintained by Eudora, until you make any changes in the future.

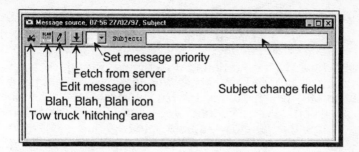

Set message priority

Fetch from server

Edit message icon   Subject change field

Blah, Blah, Blah icon

Tow truck 'hitching' area

This is the window you use for reading all your mail. As shown above, the Title bar shows a summary of the message header information, which can be useful when you are towards the bottom of a long message and cannot see the headers at the top of it.

The toolbar needs a little explanation. If you click the **Towing truck** area and drag the pointer to a mailbox icon the current open message will be moved to that mailbox immediately. If the <Ctrl> key is depressed it will be copied there.

Blah,Blah,Blah is a toggle icon that expands and contracts the display of all the message headers and formatting codes in a message. Try it out with the original message from Eudora, if you still have it.

Clicking the **Edit message** icon lets you edit the current message, maybe before you send it on to somebody else.

The **Priority** drop-down list allows you to set the importance level of a message. This is useful as you can sort on this field in the mailbox window, and rank your messages in order of importance.

The **Subject** text field lets you edit the message subject header. Some received messages have useless subject headers and this lets you change them to something more meaningful to you.

If the **Fetch** icon is selected in a message window, the entire message is downloaded the next time the server is checked for mail.

Viewing File Attachments:

Until fairly recently, e-mail on the Internet was good only for short text notes. You couldn't send attachments like formatted documents or graphics with your messages. That has now changed with the advent of MIME, which stands for Multipurpose Internet Mail Extension. With Eudora you can send formatted documents, photos, sound and video files as attachments to your main e-mail message. One thing to be careful of though, is make sure that the person you are sending attachments to has e-mail software capable of decoding them.

Incoming attachments are automatically decoded and saved on your hard disc in the Attach folder, located in the Eudora folder. Their names are displayed at the bottom of incoming messages, and to open an attachment from the message window, double-click on this name. If the application that created the attachment is installed on your computer, it will be launched with the attachment file opened in it.

Folder Maintenance

If you want to keep a message, when you have read it, you can drag it into one of the folders in the Messages window, maybe using the breakdown truck as previously described. If you do not want to keep the message clicking the **Delete** icon from the Message window will move it straight to the Trash mailbox. From a mailbox list you can delete selected messages with the **Delete** icon, or the <Del> key.

Emptying the Trash:

As you delete messages, the Trash folder of course, gets bigger and bigger over time. When you are sure you will not want any of its contained messages again, use the **Special**, **Empty Trash** command to finally remove them from your system. An alternative is to select **Empty Trash when exiting** in the **Tools**, **Options**, **Miscellaneous** setting sheet. They will then be removed whenever you close Eudora. This could be a dangerous option if you are not careful with your housekeeping.

Compressing Empty Space:

As you delete messages you create empty space on your hard disc drive and the status bar of a mailbox window shows details of the wasted space in that mailbox. To remove it you should action the **Special**, **Compact Mailboxes** menu command every now and then.

The Message Composition Window

We briefly looked into the Message Composition window earlier in the chapter. This is the window, shown below, that you will use to create any messages you want to send electronically from Eudora. It is important to understand its features, so that you can get the most out of it.

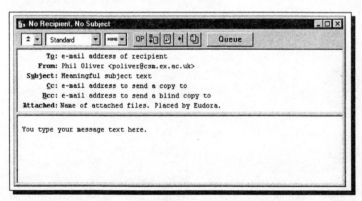

The Composition Window is opened by using the **Message**, **New Message** menu command, the

<Ctrl+N> key strokes, or by far the easiest way, by clicking the **New Message** toolbar icon shown here.

Message Recipients:

With Eudora you have a good choice of who will receive copies of any e-mail messages you send. We have described them all on the previous screen dump. Most of the fields can contain more than one address.

The Composition Window Toolbar:

Below is a brief explanation of the Composition Window toolbar. There are several icons that you will probably never need to change, we have marked these with an asterisk (*), and suggest you leave them 'depressed'.

		Sets the message priority level.
Standard		Controls the signature, if any, that is attached to the message.
MIME		Sets the type of attachment, if one is added to the message.
QP	*	Enables Quoted-printable encoding of the message.
	*	When selected, ASCII text files are attached to message, else they are included in the message.
	*	Wraps long lines of text in the message, when it is sent.
	*	Activates the <Tab> key. When this is set, it places spaces in a message.

*   When selected, a copy of the message is placed in the Out mailbox.

Send   Sends the current message, or places it in the queue.

Using Signatures:

A signature is text that can be automatically added to the bottom of a message when it is sent. This version

of Eudora offers three signature options in the Composition Window: a Standard signature, an Alternate one, or none at all.

You create the two signatures in the editor opened by the **Tools**, **Signatures**, **Standard** or **Alternate** menu command. In our example here, we want most of our messages, which are internal to our network, to be identified by a name only. When sending a message outside the building, we select the Alternate, more detailed, signature from the Composition Window toolbar.

Adding Attachments:

 If you want to send a file as an attachment to your main e-mail message, you simply click the **Attach File** toolbar button, and select the file(s) to attach from a normal Windows 95 file selection window.

The attached file's name will be placed on the **Attached:** line of the message header, as shown on the next page. You can delete this name with the <Del> key, open the file into its application program by double-clicking it, but you cannot type on this line.

113

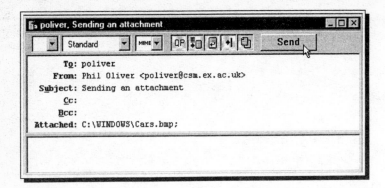

The **Attachment Type** toolbar option lets you select the format that any attachments will be encoded in, the options being MIME, or BinHex. MIME is preferable for recipients with MIME and BinHex is most compatible with old Macintosh mailers and previous versions of Eudora.

Sending Your E-mail Messages

When you have filled in the address fields, typed the body of your message and added any attachments to it, you simply click the **Send** toolbar button, shown above, to start the transmission process straight away.

If this button has **Queue** on it, the message will be held in a queue until it is sent later, as described on page 100. You should arrange your settings to queue mail if your Internet connection is by a modem, and to send it immediately if you have a permanently open connection.

If you attempt to leave Eudora without sending any queued mail, the program will warn you before exiting.

Replying to a Message

When you receive an e-mail message that you want to reply to, Eudora makes it very easy to do. The new message reply address and subject fields are both added automatically for you. Also, by default, the original message is quoted in the reply window for you to edit as required.

With the message you want to reply to open in a Message window, either click the **Reply** toolbar button, use the **Message**, **Reply** menu command, or use the <Ctrl+R> keyboard shortcut. All open the Message Composition window.

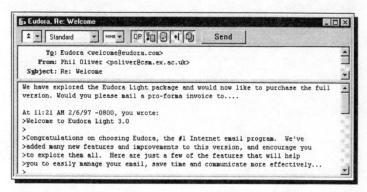

In our example above, we have set up Eudora to reply to their opening message. Note the two address fields have automatically been completed and the original message is quoted. Unfortunately the automatic signature is added to the end of the quoted part of the message, so you may be better off adding one manually.

Using Quoted Text:

It is almost an e-mail standard now to place the '>' character at the beginning of every line of quoted text in a message. Eudora does this automatically for you, as you can see above. You should not, however, leave all of the original message in your reply. This is 'not good practice', as it rapidly makes new messages very large and they can become time consuming to download. You should edit the quoted text, so that it is obvious what you are referring to. Usually one or two lines are enough.

The Address Book

E-mail addresses are often quite complicated and not easy to remember at all. With Eudora, as with all the other e-mail packages described, there is a very useful Address Book built in and an almost empty one is shown here.

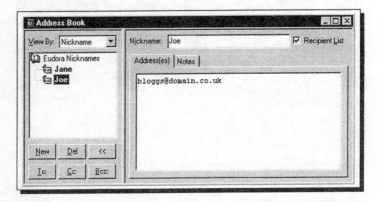

 This can be opened from any Eudora window, by clicking the **Address Book** icon, shown to the left, with the **Tools**, **Address Book** menu command, or the <Ctrl+L> key combination.

Eudora gives each person in the Address Book an alias, or Nickname. If you type a Nickname into a header field in a Message Composition Window, the program will use the correct e-mail address.

You can manually add a Nickname to the Address Book, as long as you know the e-mail address, by

clicking the **New** button. This opens the New Nickname box, shown here, where you enter a name, and opt whether to **Put it on the recipient list**.

Click **OK** and type in the open **Address(es)** field the complete e-mail address(es) of the person (or people) to be included in the nickname, separating the addresses with commas or returns. If you want, you can enter more details in the **Notes** tabbed area provided.

When you close the Address Book you are given the option to save any changes you have made to it, as shown here.

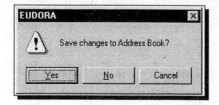

The Quick Recipient List:

The Quick Recipient List is a list of your most often-used nicknames. When you check the **Put it on the recipient list** option in an Address Book entry, it is included in the list.

To open a new message addressed to someone on your Quick Recipient List, select **New Message To**, **Forward To**, or **Redirect To** from the **Message** menu, and select the nickname from the opened list, as shown above.

To insert a nickname into an open message, put the cursor where you want the nickname and use the **Edit**, **Insert Recipient** menu command.

You can also insert the real address(es), instead of the nickname, by holding down the <Shift> key and selecting the **Edit**, **Insert Recipient** menu command.

The easiest way to add a new entry to the Address Book is to select the **Special, Make Address Book Entry** menu command. This can be used from several different locations, and is especially useful for making multiple list entries:

From the Address Book itself: highlighted entries are included in the nickname of the new entry. The **Address(es)** field will include the nicknames for the entries you selected, not the real addresses.

From a mailbox: the senders details of highlighted message(s) are included in the nickname of the new entry.

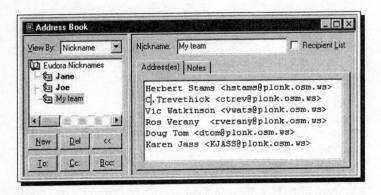

Our example above shows a multiple list entry. The 'My team' Nickname includes six people. Any message addressed to My team will be automatically sent to all of them. This is done by highlighting the Nickname in the above list and clicking the **To:** button. The **Cc:** and **Bcc:** buttons will send copies, or blind copies, to all the team members respectively.

All in all, a very useful tool, which you should experiment with until it becomes second nature.

Filtering Your Mail Messages

If you are ever in the situation of receiving e-mail messages from a regular source that you do not want to hear from, you can filter your incoming messages with Eudora. Unwanted ones can be deleted without you even having to bother with them, or messages can be automatically routed to their correct folders.

Selecting the **Tools**, **Filters** menu command opens the Filters dialogue box shown in our screen dump below. This lists the message filtering rules that have been set, and allows you to add **New** ones, and to **Remove** or edit existing ones.

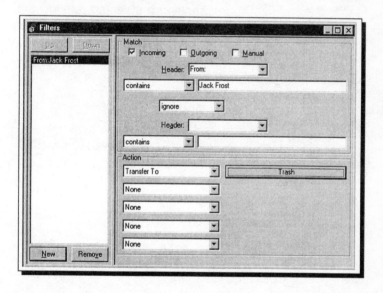

In our example above we have set up one simple filter rule that looks for messages sent **From:** a 'Jack Frost' as they are downloaded from the server mailbox. When such a message is found, it is automatically moved to the Trash mailbox.

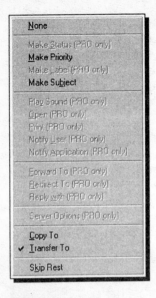

None
Make Status (PRO only)
Make Priority
Make Label (PRO only)
Make Subject
Play Sound (PRO only)
Open (PRO only)
Print (PRO only)
Notify User (PRO only)
Notify Application (PRO only)
Forward To (PRO only)
Redirect To (PRO only)
Reply with (PRO only)
Server Options (PRO only)
Copy To
✓ Transfer To
Skip Rest

If you look in one of the **Action** drop-down lists, you will find six active options that you can choose. The other eleven, shown here, are only available in the full version of Eudora Pro!

You can set multiple rules for filtering messages, but if a message matches more than one rule, then it is treated according to the first rule it matches in your list. You can change the list order by moving a selected rule **Up**, or **Down** the ranking.

The default setting in the Filters box is for **Incoming** messages to be filtered, but you can also select to filter **Outgoing** ones. The **Manual** option lets you filter selected messages in a Eudora mailbox with the **Special**, **Filter Messages** menu command.

We will leave it to you to delve deeper into this excellent facility on your own.

7. A FEW LOOSE ENDS

Mailing Lists

When you start using e-mail you want to receive lots of messages, but until your friends get active there is often a lull. This is the time to join a mailing list.

Mailing lists are automatic mailing systems where a message sent to a list address is automatically sent on to all the other members of the list. The programs that manage this automatic mailing have names like Listserv, or Majordomo, which usually form part of the List address. Some of these lists are moderated and work much like journals, where submissions are accepted, sometimes edited, and then forwarded to subscribers. Others, however, have no constraints put on their contents! Although the quality and quantity vary from list to list, you can often find a wealth of free information in them.

To subscribe to a list, you need to know the name of the list and its addresses. Commands can vary between different lists, but they often follow the format given below. Note that there is a difference between the address to which you send postings, or messages, for the list, and the address you use for subscribing to it. Be sure to distinguish between these two addresses. One of the most common mistakes made by new Internet users is to send subscription requests to list addresses, which are then forwarded to all the members on the list. Please don't make this mistake, it can be annoying and time consuming for other list readers.

List Subscription commands:

All of these commands go to the subscription address:

sub *listname First Last*   To subscribe to *listname*, with your *First* and *Last* names given.

signoff *listname*	To unsubscribe from a list.
set *listname* **nomail**	To turn off mail from a list if you are going away.
set *listname* **mail**	To turn the mail back on when you return.

Finding a Suitable List:

There are literally thousands of Mailing lists which you can join, covering almost every subject imaginable, from science, to art, to hobbies, and even ones on kinky sex. One of the biggest problems is finding the ones which interest you.

Fortunately, there are several Web sites which give details of Mailing lists. A good one we have used, which includes a search facility and many useful links should be found at

http://www.yahoo.com/Computers_and_Internet

Another one, with lists grouped by topic should be at

http://wwwneosoft.com/internet/paml/bysubj.html

Both of these will put you in direct contact with your selected lists, where you will get instructions on how to subscribe and proceed. Make sure you keep a copy of any instructions, you will need them in the future.

Once you have mastered Mailing lists you need never have an empty mailbox again.

Often Used E-mail Symbols

Once you start receiving messages from lists and other places around the globe, you may encounter some of the following acronyms, and symbols, which people often use to relieve the general boredom of life.

Acronyms:

BTW	By the way
CU	See you (bye)
FAQ	Frequently asked question
FYI	For your information
IMHO	In my humble opinion
IMO	In my opinion
ROTFL	Rolling on the floor laughing
RTFM	Read the manual!
TTYL	Talk to you later

Smileys:

You tilt your head sideways to see them:

:-)	Smiling
:-D	Laughing
;-)	Winking
:-O	Surprise
:-(	Frowning, Sad
:-I	Indifferent
:-/	Perplexed
:-{)	Smiley with a moustache
8-)	Smiley with glasses
<:-I	Dunce
:-X	My lips are sealed
:->	Sarcastic

If these appeal to you, you can get a more comprehensive selection from the *Unofficial Smiley Dictionary* reached at the following Web address:

http://www.eff.org/papers/eegtti/eeg_286.html#SEC287

E-mail Etiquette

As we saw in the first chapter, the Internet has grown up without any real control. It has grown, just like Topsy, but some of the behaviour you see there is not always quite as nice.

Parts of the media seem to have latched onto the idea that anything illegal or unusual that people get up to is because they saw how to do it on the Internet. It seems to have become something of a scapegoat. We have seen this recently regarding the making of bombs and the perpetration of credit card fraud.

The Internet does have its problem children, just like any other area of our society. Maybe one of the problems is just that, children. They seem to run wild sometimes, posting all manner of objectionable and misspelled messages.

We will very briefly mention some of the more dubious behaviour patterns you may encounter on your way round the Internet, mostly we must admit in the newsgroups, but to a lesser extent in the mailing lists as well.

Internet Flames

A flame is a particularly nasty, personal attack on somebody for something he, or she, has written in a posting. Newsgroups are notorious for flaming (burning people up). This can sometimes lead to long and drawn-out discussions on what really are stupid matters. These 'flame wars' can sometimes be fun to watch at first, but quickly grow boring, and become a general waste of everyone's time and mail space.

But, be warned, once you start posting to groups you may well upset someone, without even meaning to. If they are vicious, you may get flamed.

Spam, Spam, Bacon and Spam

Spamming, on the Internet, is the practice of sending a message to a very large number of newsgroups and mailing lists. It is named after the Monty Python sketch, where you could have what you liked in the restaurant as long as you had spam with it. A spammer gives you little choice, you have to download his posting, but you don't have to read it, though.

It will not be long before you encounter this in some form, or other. Often a product, service, or a get rich quick scheme is being offered. We tend to ignore them and hope they will go away.

Other Internet Freaks

There are a number of other types you'll soon come to recognise, and love:

Ones that think their topic of interest should be forced on everyone else as frequently as possible. Often posting dozens of messages to unrelated groups and lists, sometimes with ethnic contents.

Ones that take pages of message to get nowhere. This often includes excessive quoting by including the entire message in their reply, rather than deleting the irrelevant portions.

Ones who enjoy insulting others and post nasty, or even obscene, messages in unrelated lists.

Ones who include enormous signatures at the end of their postings, often including enormous text graphics. These are harmless, but can be annoying.

Not really in the same category, but the term 'lurker' is commonly used and needs some explanation. It usually seems to be used derogatively, but we do not know why. The best definition we have found is:

lurker:[1] */n./* One of the 'silent majority' in an electronic forum; one who posts occasionally or not at all but is known to read a group's postings regularly. This term is not pejorative and indeed is casually used reflexively: "Oh, I'm just lurking."
Often used in 'the lurkers', the hypothetical audience for the group's {flamage} - emitting regulars. When a lurker speaks up for the first time, this is called 'delurking'.

Most of us, and especially new users, must be classified as lurkers for much of the time.

Some Internet Etiquette

Often called 'netiquette' the following list, we recently found[2], makes good reading and should help you avoid most flames on the Net:

1 DON'T include the entire contents of a previous posting in your reply.

   DO cut mercilessly. Leave just enough to indicate what you're responding to. NEVER include mail headers except maybe the 'From:' line. If you can't figure out how to delete lines in your mailer software, paraphrase or re-type the quoted material.

2 DON'T reply to a point in a message without quoting or paraphrasing what you're responding to.

   DO quote (briefly) or paraphrase. If the original 'Subject:' line was 'Big dogs' make sure yours says 'Re: Big dogs'. Some REPLY functions do this automatically. By net convention, included lines are preceded by '>' (greater-than signs).

---

[1]   The on-line hacker Jargon File, version 3.3.3, 25 MAR 1996
[2]   Patrick Crispen's Internet Roadmap, 1994

126

All the mail editors we describe do this automatically. Others require you to do it manually or set the 'indent character' to '>'.

3   DON'T send lines longer than 70 characters. This is a kindness to folks with terminal-based mail editors. Some mail gateways truncate extra characters turning your deathless prose into gibberish.

Some mail editor tools only SEEM to insert line breaks for you, but actually don't, so that every paragraph is one immense line. Learn what your mail editor does.

4   DON'T SEND A MESSAGE IN ALL CAPS. CAPITALISED MESSAGES ARE HARDER TO READ THAN LOWER CASE OR MIXED CASE.

DO use normal capitalisation. Separate your paragraphs with blank lines. Make your message inviting to your potential readers.

5   DON'T betray confidences. It is all too easy to quote a personal message and regret it.

DO read the 'To:' and 'Cc:' lines in your message before you send it. Are you SURE you want the mail to go there?

6   DON'T make statements which can be interpreted as official positions of your organisation or offers to do business. Saying "Boy, I'd sure like to have one of them Crays" could result in a truck at your loading dock and a bill in the mail even larger than a student loan.

DO treat every post as though you were sending a copy to your boss, your minister, and your worst enemy.

7 DON'T rely on the ability of your readers to tell the difference between serious statements and satire, or sarcasm. It's hard to write funny. It's even harder to write satire.

DO remember that no one can hear your tone of voice. Use smileys, like:

:-) or **;^)**

turn your head anti-clockwise to see the smile.

You can also use capitals for emphasis, or use Net conventions for italics and underlines as in: "You said the guitar solo on "Comfortably Numb" from Pink Floyd's, The Wall, was *lame*? Are you OUT OF YOUR MIND???!!!"

8 DON'T send a message that says nothing but "Me, too", or something equally as trivial. This is most annoying when combined with (1) or (2) above. Another one is "I don't know."

DO remember the immortal words of Martin Farquhar Tupper (1810-1889): *"Well-timed silence hath more eloquence than speech."*

8. GLOSSARY OF TERMS

Agent
A search tool that automatically seeks out relevant on-line information.

Anonymous ftp
Anonymous ftp allows you to connect to a remote computer and transfer public files back to your local computer without the need to have a user ID and password.

Application
Software (program) designed to carry out certain activity, such as word processing.

Archie
Archie is an Internet service that allows you to locate files that can be downloaded via FTP.

Association
An identification of a filename extension to a program. This lets Windows open the program when its files are selected.

ASCII
A binary code representation of a character set. The name stands for 'American Standard Code for Information Interchange'.

Attributes
Indicate whether a file is read-only, hidden or system and if it has changed since it was last backed up.

Backup
To make a back-up copy of a file or a disc for safekeeping.

Bandwidth
The range of transmission frequencies a network can use. The greater the bandwidth the more information that can be transferred over a network.

Base memory	The first 1 MB of random access memory.
Batch file	An ASCII formatted file that contains DOS commands which can be executed by the computer.
Baud	The unit of measurement used to describe data transmission speed. One baud is one bit per second.
BBS	Bulletin Board System, a computer equipped with software and telecoms links that allow it to act as an information host for remote computer systems.
BinHex	A file conversion format that converts binary files to ASCII text files.
BIOS	The Basic Input/Output System. It allows the core of a PC's operating system to communicate with the hardware.
Bit	A binary digit; the smallest unit of information that can be stored, either as a 1 or as a 0.
Bitmap	A technique for managing the image displayed on a computer screen.
Browse	A button in some Windows dialogue boxes that lets you view a list of files and folders before you make a selection.
Browser	A program, like the Internet Explorer, that lets you graphically view World Wide Web pages.
Buffer	RAM memory allocated to store data being read from disc.

Byte	A grouping of binary digits (0 or 1) which represent information.
Cache	An area of memory, or disc space, reserved for data, which speeds up down-loading.
Card	A removable printed-circuit board that is plugged into a computer expansion slot.
CD-ROM	Compact Disk - Read Only Memory; an optical disc from which information may be read but not written.
Check box	A small box in a dialogue box that can be selected (X), or cleared (empty).
Click	To quickly press and release a mouse button.
Client	A computer that has access to services over a computer network. The computer providing the services is a server.
Client application	A Windows application that can accept linked, or embedded, objects.
Clipboard	A temporary storage area of memory, where text and graphics are stored with the Windows cut and copy actions.
Close	To remove a dialogue box or window, or to exit a program.
Code page	A table in Windows that defines which extended ASCII character set is used in a document.
Command	An instruction given to a computer to carry out a particular action.

Command line	The line in an MS-DOS window, or screen, into which you enter DOS commands.
Command Prompt	The prompt (e.g. C>) which appears on the command line to let you know that DOS is ready to receive a command.
Computer name	The name that identifies a specific computer to other users of a network.
Configuration	A general purpose term referring to the way you have your computer set up.
CONFIG.SYS	A special file that allows the system to be configured to your requirements.
CPU	The Central Processing Unit; the main chip that executes all instructions entered into a computer.
Cyberspace	Originated by William Gibson in his novel "Neuromancer", now used to describe the Internet and the other computer networks.
DDE	Dynamic data exchange - a process that enables you to exchange data between two or more Windows programs.
Dial-up Connection	A popular form of Net connection for the home user, over standard telephone lines.
Direct Connection	A permanent connection between your computer system and the Internet. Often referred to as a leased-line connection.

Default	The command, device or option automatically chosen.
Desktop	The Windows screen working background, on which you place icons, folders, etc.
Device driver	A special file that must be loaded into memory for Windows to be able to address a specific procedure or hardware device.
Device name	A logical name used by DOS to identify a device, such as LPT1 or COM1 for the parallel or serial printer.
Dialogue box	A window displayed on the screen to allow the user to enter information.
Dimmed	Unavailable menu options shown in a different colour.
Directory	An area on disc where information relating to a group of files is kept. Known as a folder in Windows 95.
Disc	A device on which you can store programs and data.
Disc file	A collection of program code, or data, that is stored under a given name on a disc.
Disconnect	To detach a drive, port or computer from a shared device, or to break an Internet connection.
Document	When used in reference to the Web, a document is any file containing text, media or hyperlinks that can be transferred from an HTTP server to a browser.

	Otherwise it is a file produced by an application program.
Domain	A group of devices, servers and computers on a network.
DOS	Disc Operating System. A collection of small specialised programs that allow interaction between user and computer.
DOS prompt	The prompt displayed in an MS-DOS window, or screen, such as A> or C>, indicating that DOS is ready to accept commands.
Double-click	To quickly press and release a mouse button twice.
Download	To transfer to your computer a file, or data, from another computer.
DPI	Dots Per Inch - a resolution standard for laser printers.
Drag	To move an object on the screen by pressing and holding down the left mouse button while moving the mouse.
Drive name	The letter followed by a colon which identifies a floppy or hard disc drive.
EISA	Extended Industry Standard Architecture, for construction of PCs with the Intel 32 bit microprocessor.
Embedded object	Information in a document that is 'copied' from its source application. Selecting the object opens the creating application from within the document.

Enter key	The key that is pressed after entering data on the command line.
Expanded memory	This is memory outside the conventional RAM (first 640 KB) and is used by some MS-DOS software to store data and run applications.
Extended memory	This is memory above the 1-MB memory address, all of which is used by Windows 95.
FAQ	Acronym for Frequently Asked Questions. A common feature on the Internet, FAQs are files of answers to commonly asked questions.
FAT	The File Allocation Table. An area on disc where information is kept on which part of the disc a file is located.
File extension	The optional suffix following the period in a filename. Windows uses this to identify the source application program.
Filename	The name given to a file. In Windows 95 this can be up to 256 characters long.
Filespec	File specification made up of drive, path and filename.
Firewall	Security measures designed to protect a networked system from unauthorised access.
Fixed disc	The hard disc of a computer.

Floppy disc	A removable disc on which information can be stored magnetically.
Folder	An area used to store a group of files, usually with a common link.
Font	A graphic design representing a set of characters, numbers and symbols.
Formatting	The process of preparing a disc so that it can store information, or of controlling the visual layout of a document.
FTP	File Transfer Protocol. The procedure for connecting to a remote computer and transferring files back to your local computer.
Function key	One of the series of 10 or 12 keys marked with the letter F and a numeral, used for specific operations.
Gopher	A text oriented, hierarchically organised, tool used to locate online resources.
Graphics card	A device that controls the display on the monitor and other allied functions.
GUI	A Graphic User Interface, such as Windows 95, the software front-end meant to provide an attractive and easy to use interface.
Hardcopy	Output on paper.
Hard disc	A device built into the computer for holding programs and data.

Hardware	The equipment that makes up a computer system, excluding the programs or software.
Help	A Windows system that gives you instructions and additional information on using a program.
Highlight	The change to a reverse-video appearance when a menu item or area of text is selected.
HMA	High Memory Area; the first 64 KB of memory beyond the end of the base memory.
Home Page	The document displayed when you first open your Web browser, or the first document you come to at a Web site.
Hotlist	A list of frequently used Web locations and URL addresses.
Host	A computer acting as an information or communications server.
HTML	HyperText Markup Language, the format used in documents on the World Wide Web.
HTTP	HyperText Transport Protocol the system used to link and transfer hypertext documents on the Web.
Hypermedia	Hypertext extended to include linked multi-media.
Hypertext	A system that allows documents to be cross-linked so that the reader can explore related links, or documents, by clicking on a highlighted word or symbol.

Icon	A small graphic image that represents a function or object. Clicking on an icon produces an action.
Insertion point	A flashing bar that shows where typed text will be entered into a document.
Interface	A device that allows you to connect a computer to its peripherals.
Internet	The global system of computer networks.
IRQ	Interrupt request lines - hardware lines used by devices to signal the processor that they are ready to send, or receive, data.
ISA	Industry Standard Architecture; a standard for internal connections in PCs.
ISDN	Integrated Services Digital Network, a telecom standard using digital transmission technology to support voice, video and data communications applications over regular telephone lines.
Key combination	When two or more keys are pressed simultaneously, such as <Ctrl+Esc>.
Kilobyte	(KB); 1024 bytes of information or storage space.
LAN	Local Area Network; PCs, workstations or minis sharing files and peripherals within the same site.

LCD	Liquid Crystal Display.
Linked object	A placeholder for an object inserted into a destination document.
Links	The hypertext connections between Web pages.
Local	A resource that is located on your computer, not linked to it over a network.
Log on	To gain access to a network.
Long filename	In Windows 95 the name given to a file can be up to 256 characters long.
MAPI	Messaging Application Program Interface - an interface that lets you send e-mail messages from any MAPI-compatible application, such as a word processor or spreadsheet.
MCA	Micro Channel Architecture; IBM's standard for construction of PCs introduced in the 1990s.
MCI	Media Control Interface - a standard for files and multi-media devices.
Megabyte	(MB); 1024 kilobytes of information or storage space.
Megahertz	(MHz); Speed of processor in millions of cycles per second.
Memory	Part of computer consisting of storage elements organised into addressable locations that can hold data and instructions.

Menu	A list of available options in an application.
Menu bar	The horizontal bar that lists the names of menus.
Microprocessor	The calculating chip within a computer.
MIDI	Musical Instrument Digital Interface - enable devices to transmit and receive sound and music messages.
MIME	Multipurpose Internet Mail Extensions, a messaging standard that allows Internet users to exchange e-mail messages enhanced with graphics, video and voice.
MIPS	Million Instructions Per Second.
Mouse	A device used to manipulate a pointer around your display and activate processes by pressing buttons.
MS-DOS	Microsoft's implementation of the Disc Operating System for PCs.
Multimedia	The use of photographs, music and sound and movie images in a presentation.
Multi-tasking	Performing more than one operation at the same time.
NCSA	National Center for Super-computing Applications, in US.
Network	A computer network is an inter-connection of computers allowing the exchange and sharing of resources (files, data, computing power).

Network server	Central computer which stores files for several linked computers.
Node	A device attached to a network, which uses the network as a means of communication and has an address on the network.
Novell MHS	Novell's messaging system.
Operating System	A group of programs that translates your commands to the computer.
Page	A Web page, as used in a browser, is the entire document, however long.
Password	A unique character string used to gain access to a network, program, or mailbox.
PATH	The location of a file in the directory tree.
Peripheral	Any device attached to a PC.
PIF file	Program information file - gives information to Windows about an MS-DOS application.
Pixel	A picture element on screen; the smallest element that can be independently assigned colour and intensity.
POP3	Post Office Protocol 3 is an Internet standard which defines a mechanism for accessing a mailbox located on a remote host machine.
Port	An input/output address through which your PC interacts with external devices.

PPP	Point-to-Point Protocol, a connection where phone lines and a modem can be used to connect to the Internet.
Print queue	A list of print jobs waiting to be sent to a printer.
Program	A set of instructions which cause a computer to perform tasks.
Prompt	The MS-DOS prompt displayed on the command line, such as A> or C>, indicating that DOS is ready to accept commands.
Protected mode	The operating mode of 386 (and higher) processors, which allows more than 1 MB of memory to be addressed.
Protocol	A set of standards that define how traffic and communications are handled by a computer or network routers. The specific protocol used on the Internet is TCP/IP.
PS/2	The range of PCs first introduced by IBM in late 1980s.
RAM	Random Access Memory. The computer's volatile memory. Data held in it is lost when power is switched off.
Real mode	MS-DOS mode, typically used to run programs, such as MS-DOS games, that will not run under Windows.
Resource	A directory, or printer, that can be shared over a network.
Right-click	To click and release the right mouse button, which often opens

a context sensitive menu in a Windows application.

ROM

Read Only Memory. A PC's non-volatile memory. Data is written into this memory at manufacture and is not affected by power loss.

Root directory

The main disc directory under which a number of sub-directories can be created.

Router

A communications device used to transmit over a network via the most efficient route possible.

Screen saver

A display program that moves images on an inactive screen.

Scroll bar

A bar that appears at the right side or bottom edge of a window.

Search Engine

A program that helps users find information across the Internet.

Sector

Disc space, normally 512 bytes long.

Serial interface

An interface that transfers data as individual bits; each operation has to be completed before the next starts.

Server

A computer system that manages and delivers information for client computers.

Shared resource

Any device, program or file that is available to network users.

Shareware

Software that is available on public networks and bulletin boards. Users are expected to pay a nominal amount to the software developer.

143

Site	A server, or a collection of linked Web pages at a single location.
Software	The programs and instructions that control your PC.
SLIP	Serial Line Internet Protocol, a method of Internet connection that enables computers to use phone lines and a modem to connect to the Internet without having to connect to a host.
SMTP	Simple Mail Transfer Protocol, is the standard mechanism by which mail is delivered on the Internet and on TCP/IP networks.
Socket	An end-point for sending and receiving data between computers.
Spooler	Software which handles transfer of information to a store where it will be used by a peripheral device.
SSL	Secure Sockets Layer, the standard transmission security protocol developed by Netscape, which has been put into the public domain.
SVGA	Super Video Graphics Array; it has all the VGA modes but with 256, or more, colours.
System disc	A disc containing files to enable MS-DOS to start up.
Tags	Formatting codes used in HTML documents, which indicate how parts of a document will appear when displayed.

TCP/IP	Transmission Control Protocol /Internet Protocol, combined protocols that perform the transfer of data between two computers. TCP monitors and ensures the correct transfer of data. IP receives the data, breaks it up into packets, and sends it to a network within the Internet.
Telnet	A program which allows users to remotely use computers across networks.
Text file	An unformatted file of text characters saved in ASCII format.
Toolbar	A bar containing icons giving quick access to commands.
Toggle	To turn an action on and off with the same switch.
TrueType fonts	Fonts that can be scaled to any size and print as they show on the screen.
UMB	A block of upper memory made available by a 386 memory manager into which memory resident software can be loaded.
Upper memory	The 384 KB of memory between the top of conventional memory and the end of the base memory.
URL	Uniform Resource Locator, the addressing system used on the Web, containing information about the method of access, the server to be accessed and the path of the file to be accessed.
User ID	A one-word name used to identify a specific user of a specific

	computer or network. Usually assigned by the system administrator and often includes a portion of the individual's name.
Usenet	The global news-reading network.
Veronica	A search utility that helps find information on gopher servers.
Virtual machine	A logical computer that Windows 95 creates in memory.
Virtual memory	See swap file.
Volume label	An identifying label written to a disc when it is first formatted.
WAIS	Wide Area Information Service, a Net-wide system for looking up specific information in Internet databases.
Web	See World Wide Web.
Web Page	An HTML document that is accessible on the Web.
Wildcard character	A character that can be included in a filename to indicate any other character (?), or group of characters (*).
World Wide Web	A network of hypertext-based multimedia information servers. Web browsers, such as the Internet Explorer, can be used to view any information on the Web.
Zine	An electronic magazine accessed through the Web.

APPENDIX - KEYBOARD SHORTCUTS

The actions described below are the standard keyboard shortcuts for the four e-mail programs described in the book.

Keyboard Shortcuts for Pegasus Mail

Shortcut	Action
Shortcut	*Action*
Ctrl + A	Select all
Ctrl + C	Copy to clipboard
Ctrl + F	Find text
Ctrl + G	Find again
Ctrl + K	Check spelling
Ctrl + L	Mail folders
Ctrl + N	New message
Ctrl + P	Print message
Ctrl + R	Find and replace
Ctrl + V	Paste from clipboard
Ctrl + W	Read new mail
Ctrl + X	Cut to clipboard
Ctrl + Z	Undo
F1	Open Help
F2	Local users
F3	Address books
Shift + F3	Quick lookup
F4	Logged in users
Shift + F4	Enlarge window
Alt + F4	Close Pegasus
F6	Distribution lists
Shift + F10	Open Options settings
F11	Set colour in folder

Keyboard Shortcuts for Netscape Mail

Shortcut	Action
Ctrl + A	Selects all
Ctrl + B	Bookmarks
Shift + Ctrl + A	Selects message thread
Ctrl + C	Copies the present selection to the clipboard
Ctrl + E	Redoes the last undo action performed
Ctrl + F	Finds a word or phrase
Ctrl + H	Send messages in Outbox
Ctrl + K	Compress mail folder
Ctrl + L	Forwards a message
Ctrl + M	Opens a new e-mail window to create and send a new message
Ctrl + N	Open new Web browser page
Ctrl + P	Prints current message
Ctrl + R	Replies to a message
Shift + Ctrl + R	Replies to all recipients of a message
Ctrl + S	Starts the Save As procedure, to save a message to a disc file
Ctrl + T	Gets new mail
Ctrl + V	Pastes the clipboard contents
Ctrl + W	Close the Mail program
Ctrl + X	Cuts to the clipboard
Ctrl + Z	Undoes the last action performed
Esc	Stops loading the current page
Del	Delete message
F3	Finds the next occurrence of the word or phrase used in the last Find operation

Keyboard Shortcuts for MS Explorer Mail

Shortcut	*Action*
General	
F1	Open help topics
Ctrl + A	Select All
Main Mail Window	
Ctrl + O	Open the selected message
Ctrl + Space	Mark a message as read
Tab	Move between window panes
Main and Read Message Windows	
Ctrl + D	Delete a message
Ctrl + F	Forward a message
Ctrl + I	Go to your Inbox
Ctrl + M	Send and receive mail
Ctrl + N	Open a new message
Ctrl + P	Print the selected message
Ctrl + R	Reply to the author
Shift + Ctrl + R	Reply to all
Ctrl + >	Go to next message in the list
Ctrl + <	Go to previous message in the list
Alt + Enter	View properties of selected message
Send Message Window	
F3	Find text
Esc	Close a message
Ctrl + K	Check names
Ctrl + Enter	Send a message

Keyboard Shortcuts for Eudora Light

Shortcut	*Action*
Ctrl + 0	Open the Out mailbox
Ctrl + 1	Open the In mailbox
Ctrl + '	Paste as quotation
Ctrl + ,	Finish nickname
Ctrl + A	Select all
Ctrl + C	Copy to clipboard
Ctrl + D	Delete
Ctrl + E	Send or Queue
Ctrl + F	Opens Find dialogue box
Ctrl + H	Attach document
Ctrl + J	Filter messages
Ctrl + K	Make nickname
Ctrl + L	Opens Address Book
Ctrl + M	Check mail
Ctrl + N	New message
Ctrl + O	Open file
Ctrl + P	Print
Ctrl + Q	Exit Eudora
Ctrl + R	Reply
Ctrl + S	Save
Ctrl + T	Send queued messages
Ctrl + V	Paste to clipboard
Ctrl + W	Close message
Ctrl + X	Cut to clipboard
Ctrl + Y	Directory Services
Ctrl + Z	Undo
Shift + Send	Open the Change Queuing dialogue box
Shift + Open	Open the selected message with all headers displayed
Shift + Sort	Sort in descending order
Shift + Transfer	Put a copy of the current message in the selected mailbox and leave the original where it is

Shift + Copy	Copy the selected text without the carriage returns (copy unwrapped)
Shift + Paste	Paste the selection as plain text, but do not paste the style information
Shift + Wrap	Remove the carriage returns from the selected text (unwrap)
Shift + Exit	Set all currently open windows to open again when Eudora is next started
Shift + Save	Save changes to all open windows
Shift + Close	Close all open windows
Arrows	Move from one message to another in a mailbox, depending on the Miscellaneous Option settings
Enter	Select the outlined button in any dialogue box, alert, or window, or open the selected messages or URL
Esc	Stop any operation currently in progress
F1	Display Help
Page Up	Scroll up through the window
Page Down	Scroll down through the window

INDEX

NOTES

NOTES

COMPANION DISCS

There is no COMPANION DISC for this book.

COMPANION DISCS for many of the other computer books written by the same author(s) and published by BERNARD BABANI (publishing) LTD, except for the ones with an asterisk against their title in the list at the front of this book, are available.

Make sure you fill in your name and address and specify the book number and title in your order.

ORDERING INSTRUCTIONS
To obtain companion discs, fill in the order form below, or a copy of it if you don't want to spoil your book, enclose a cheque (payable to **P.R.M. Oliver**) or a postal order, and send it to the address given below.

Book No.	Book Name	Unit Price	Total Price
BP		£3.50	
BP		£3.50	
BP		£3.50	
Name .... Address		Sub-total	£.............
		P & P (@ 45p/disc)	£.............
		Total Due	£.............
Send to: P.R.M. Oliver, CSM, Pool, Redruth, Cornwall, TR15 3SE			

PLEASE NOTE
The author(s) are fully responsible for providing this Companion Disc service. The publishers of this book accept no responsibility for the supply, quality, or magnetic contents of the disc, or in respect of any damage, or injury that might be suffered or caused by its use.